QuickBooks Online for Beginners, Updated Edition

A Complete and Easy-to-Follow Guide to Master Bookkeeping for Small Business Owners

Steven Carlson

TABLE OF CONTENTS

01. **INTRODUCTION** 8

02. **THE BASICS OF QUICKBOOKS** 10
    What is QuickBooks and What is it Used for 10
    What are the Different Versions of QuickBooks 11
    Which Edition of QuickBooks Online is Right for You 12

03. **FIRST STEPS** 17
    How to Set Up QuickBooks for Business 27
    How to Add New Customers 28
    How to Add New Products and Services 31
    How to Set up Chart of Accounts 34
    Importing spreadsheets and desktop data 37

04. **ACCOUNTING** 40
    How to connect a bank account or credit card 40
    Understanding the Bank Feeds 45
    Create a Rule and Split Transactions 50
    Reconciling an Account. What it is for and How do you do it .. 53
    How to Invite an Accountant to View your Account 56

05. **EXPENSES** 59
    How to Add New Suppliers 59
    How to Add Expenses and What are the Types of Expenses ... 61
    How to Manage Expenses 65
    How to Record Check 66
    Add Bills and Bill Payments 68

06. **INVOICING** 71
    Create and Customize and Invoice 71
    How to Send Invoice Reminders 74

07. SALES AND REFUNDS 77
Receive and Record Invoice Payments 77
What is Undeposited Funds account and how is it used? 79
Record a bank deposit 80
Record a Refund 81
How to Record a Supplier Refund 84

08. PAYROLL 88
How to Set Up Payroll and Add Employees 88
How to Pay Employees Using Direct Deposit 91
Creating a Timesheet for Employees 94

09. TRACKING & MANAGEMENT 97
How to Start Tracking your Stock 98
How to Reorder Inventory from Vendors When Low on Stock 99
How to Create Projects and Start Tracking Them 101

10. TAXES   110
Adding VAT 110
Creating and filing 1099s 113

11. Reports   117
Types of Report 117
Add a Report as Favorite 119
Most Important Types of Statements 119
How to Customize Reports 122

12. Trouble Shooting 126
Most common errors in QuickBooks and how to fix them 126

13. CONCLUSION 133

We invite you to scan this **QR code** using the camera of your phone to access your bonus content:

SCAN THE QR CODE BELOW

You will find **useful invoice templates** you can use with Quick-books, as well as your two complementary ebooks **Accounting 101** and **Time Management For Entrepreneurs**

© Copyright 2022 - All rights reserved.

The content contained within this book may not be reproduced, duplicated or transmitted without direct written permission from the author or the publisher. Under no circumstances will any blame or legal responsibility be held against the publisher, or author, for any damages, reparation, or monetary loss due to the information contained within this book, either directly or indirectly.

Legal Notice:

This book is copyright protected. It is only for personal use. You cannot amend, distribute, sell, use, quote or paraphrase any part, or the content within this book, without the consent of the author or publisher.

INTRODUCTION

If you are a business owner, you will have to deal with one of the most important elements of running your business: bookkeeping. This and other company obligations might be burdensome. You want your firm to run properly, so you are learning from QuickBooks Online, one of the most popular accounting software for small businesses. With more than 5.3 million users, QuickBooks has gained a reputation for being easy to use. However, it is not as simple as many people think.

If you are new to QuickBooks, it may feel like a maze. Learning takes time, which busy people like you do not have. Other QuickBooks Online lessons utilize too many technical terms, which is confusing. It is frustrating to read multiple resources that only provide limited QuickBooks information.

Because of all these things, you might be wasting money by not getting the full benefit of what you buy for the bookkeeping needs of your business. What is more, you could miss maximizing on a promising product that will help you improve your understanding of accounting to do your job better.

Fortunately, we have the perfect guide for you!

QuickBooks Online for Beginners, Updated Edition, makes it simple for you to understand and learn how to use QuickBooks Online. This book is perfect for business owners or brand-new users who are still getting to know the concepts of accounting and bookkeeping. It is also great for anyone with a little knowledge of accounting principles who would like to get started now instead of waiting any longer.

The tutorials will walk you through exactly what you need to know to get started with QuickBooks Online, including how to set up an account, record transactions, generate reports and invoices, manage bills, reconcile bank accounts, track expenses, and pay bills efficiently.

QUICKBOOKS ONLINE
FOR BEGINNERS, UPDATED EDITION

This book is complete with details and thorough instructions to get you ahead in using this popular cloud accounting software, so you do not need to consult other sources. Plus, we do not want to overwhelm you with too much information that is not useful to you. We want it to be as easy as possible while meeting your expectations for your business needs.

Taking everything into consideration, it is not surprising why QuickBooks Online for Beginners, Updated Edition, is loved by many.

If you are just getting started with QuickBooks Online, now is the best time to get this book and use it as a guide to learn how to use the software. But if you have subscribed previously and are still not taking advantage of this book, then this is your second-best chance to download it and start browsing to get the hang of it in no time. Do not miss the path to becoming a QuickBooks Online champion.

Get your copy now and start learning the basics of this popular accounting software right away. Start growing your business today!

01
THE BASICS OF QUICKBOOKS

WHAT IS QUICKBOOKS AND WHAT IS IT USED FOR

QuickBooks is a comprehensive accounting and business management solution ideal for small businesses. You can automate many of your bookkeeping tasks and receive detailed overviews of your business's financial health.

It comes with a variety of helpful features, such as online accounting, inventory tracking, and invoicing, so you can keep track of your company's expenses and profits. QuickBooks can also save you money by helping you reduce paper waste and manpower costs while increasing efficiency.

QuickBooks is a popular accounting software you can use to help you with the following:

Invoicing

QuickBooks automates the invoicing and collection processes for your business, which is much faster than doing it on paper. You can also customize professional-looking invoices and easily set up an automated payment process to get paid faster.

Tracking your expenses

The fastest way to take control of your business expenses, from anywhere. QuickBooks organizes and brings together all of your business's financial information, while spending less time posting receipts and tracking expenses.

Get insights into your finances

Getting a quick snapshot of how your business is performing with smart insights is just a click away. Generate insightful reports and manage your cash flow in real-time to help you analyze risks and make smarter decisions about your businesses.

Tax obligations

You can save time and money on taxes as QuickBooks automatically calculates your tax deductions. You can also track and report Goods and Services Tax (GST), Value-Added Tax (VAT), sales tax, and other taxes in one place.

Inventory

QuickBooks syncs with online sales platforms to help you manage your stock effectively. It gives you a clear picture of what is selling and what is not, so you can manage inventory more effectively before it has gotten out of date.

WHAT ARE THE DIFFERENT VERSIONS OF QUICKBOOKS

There are several QuickBooks products available that are categorized as online and desktop versions with each having different editions right for your type of business.

1. QuickBooks Online

QuickBooks Online is an easy-to-use, cloud-based accounting software, which means you can work with this product from any place with an internet connection. It is convenient to use because its data is safely stored online and has an available mobile app, so it allows you to switch to multiple devices.

QuickBooks Online has impressive automation and bookkeeping tools, including income and expense tracking, tax management, invoicing, and bill payments. This online version is available in four editions that will be discussed later.

2. QuickBooks Desktop

- QuickBooks Pro

    For new business owners or small enterprises that prefer a desktop application, QuickBooks Pro is recommended. This product is the most basic desktop version of QuickBooks and delivers up to three users at a time. Some of its strong features include accounts payable, managing and paying bills, and inventory tracking.

- QuickBooks Premier

    QuickBooks Premier is another locally installed application that gives five users access. It shares the same functionalities as QuickBooks Pro, but what sets it apart are the features that are suitable for industry-specific businesses such as contractors, manufacturers, and nonprofits.

- QuickBooks Enterprise

    With up to 40 users, QuickBooks Enterprise is suitable for larger businesses requiring robust tools and features. QuickBooks Enterprise is also a desktop software with a capacity similar to that of Pro and Premier but is the most powerful version because of its advanced inventory, complex financial reporting, and more.

- QuickBooks for Mac

    A QuickBooks desktop version specifically designed for Mac computers is also available. Mac users can take advantage of syncing with Mac OS address books and iCal calendars, right from QuickBooks for Mac and with accounting features also like QuickBooks Pro for Windows.

WHICH EDITION OF QUICKBOOKS ONLINE IS RIGHT FOR YOU

With over 650 integrations, powerful features, and strong security, QuickBooks Online is considered the best option for small businesses overall. This cloud-based software offers different editions that include specific bookkeeping features and tools designed to meet your requirements.

1. QuickBooks Online Self-Employed

If you are an independent contractor or a self-starter in a business that needs basic tax support, QuickBooks Online Self-Employed is the ideal plan for you. QuickBooks Self Employed helps you file Schedule C,

It tracks your income, organizes your receipts, and imports your business expenses directly from your bank accounts to help you get ready for the tax season. This software comes with all of the features you need to manage your expenses, run financial reports, and even track the mileage of your business trips.

Inclusions:

- Income and expense tracking
- Reports generation
- Receipt capture
- Mileage tracking
- Tax deductions
- Estimate taxes
- File taxes

QuickBooks Online Self-Employed has three different versions from which you can choose.

- Self-Employed – includes basic bookkeeping tools

    Features:

    - Separate business and personal expenses
    - Schedule C deductions
    - Automatic estimation of quarterly taxes
    - Mileage tracking

- **Self-Employed Tax Bundle** – comes with Intuit TurboTax Self-Employed tax software for self-employed

    Features:

    - All Self-Employed features
    - Direct payment of quarterly taxes using QuickBooks
    - Transfer into TurboTax
    - With one state and one federal tax return filing

- **Self-Employed Live Tax Bundle** – with Intuit TurboTax Live Self-Employed that offers support from a CPA aside from the use of tax software

    Features:

    - All Self-Employed Tax Bundle features
    - Consultation with CPAs
    - All year unrestricted assistance and advice available
    - Final review of your tax return with a CPA

2. QuickBooks Online Simple Start

QuickBooks Simple Start is best for single users, such as freelancers and solo entrepreneurs. It is budget-friendly and lets you easily manage costs, invoices, track payments and expenses, categorize transactions, automate sales taxes, and more. QuickBooks Simple Start is a simple tool, so doing basic bookkeeping yourself is easy.

Inclusions:

- Income and expense tracking
- Invoices and payments
- Tax deductions
- Run reports
- Receipt capture
- Mileage tracking
- Cash flow
- Sales and sales tax tracking
- Create estimates
- Manage contractors

3. QuickBooks Online Essentials

QuickBooks Online Essentials comes with up to three users and gives you all the features of QuickBooks Simple Start plus the ability to manage where you can track your bills, set recurring payments, and pay multiple vendors and bills at the same time. If you have a service-based business, this plan is a good fit for you because it can automate adding billable hours of work or services to invoices.

Inclusions:

- All Simple Start features
- Includes three users
- Bill management
- Time tracking

4. QuickBooks Online Plus

With QuickBooks Online Plus, you can achieve all the functionality the QuickBooks Online Essentials offers with additional features such as project profitability and tracking of inventory and stocks.

Businesses that sell products, such as retailers and wholesalers, benefit the most from QuickBooks Online Plus. Contractors can also benefit from this plan by monitoring the profits from their services. Additionally, QuickBooks Online Plus simplifies the tracking of payroll, labor costs, and expenses with job costing and allows five account users.

Inclusions:

- All Simple Start and Essentials features
- Up to five users
- Inventory tracking
- Project profitability

5. QuickBooks Online Advanced

If you need powerful accounting that improves the business processes of your growing company, then QuickBooks Online Advanced is the right fit for you. QuickBooks Online Advanced is designed to help you run your business with large transactions more efficiently.

It offers smart features like batch invoicing, custom user roles, automated workflows, premium support, app integrations, and more. QuickBooks Online Advanced is a robust solution to help you maximize business productivity, allowing up to 25 users for easy collaboration.

Inclusions:

- All Simple Start, Essentials, and Plus features
- Up to 25 users
- Business analytics with Excel
- Employee expenses
- Batch invoices and expenses
- Customized access
- Exclusive premium apps
- Dedicated account team
- On-demand training
- Workflow automation
- Data restoration

02
FIRST STEPS

Getting started with QuickBooks is easy. With its simple and intuitive interface, you can save time, money, and stress while creating and managing your bookkeeping tasks.

QuickBooks provides a range of tools and features you can easily see right after logging in to simplify your day-to-day tasks so that you can focus on what matters most, helping your business grow.

The QuickBooks dashboard gives you the look and feel of a smart accounting display. There are a variety of tabs, buttons, and links put together on the dashboard so you can locate your needs easily.

This page is divided into headers, a side navigation pane, as well as two main dashboard categories, "Get things done" and "Business overview."

Let us run through the different sections and functions of the dashboard.

The Header

This area of the dashboard is located at the top and is composed of helpful icons for a better user experience.

Triple bar icon – This shows the full screen of the dashboard without the sidebar menu.

Company name and logo – This is where your company name and logo appear.

Help – The help button lets you search questions or contact support to get live assistance.

- Search questions, and type in keywords or topics. You can also click **Contact Us** to get further support. Use the QuickBooks Assistant feature for your custom queries and get real-time assistance.

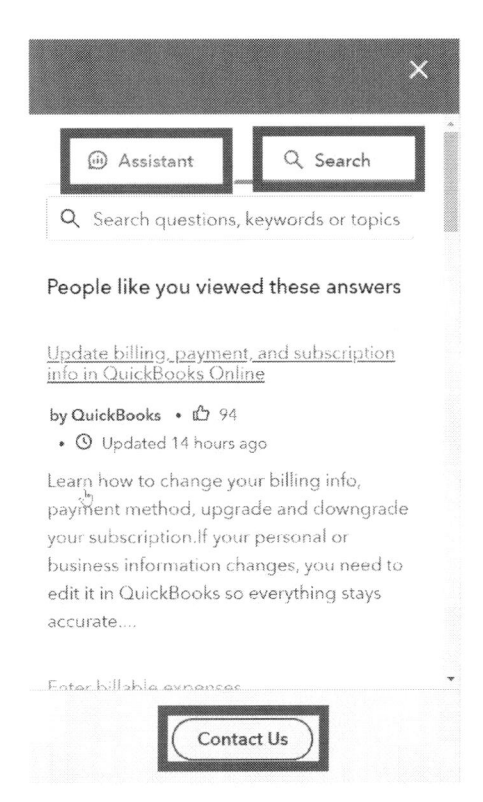

Magnifying glass – This icon is where you can search for your recent transactions or records in your account.

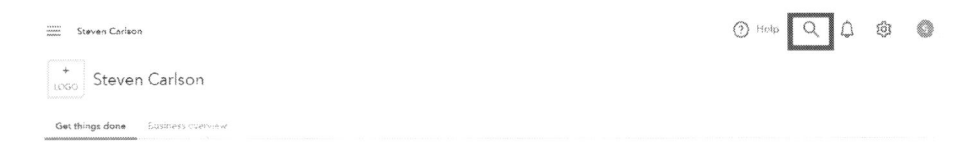

- Search using the tips for faster results or try **Advanced Search** for detailed search results.

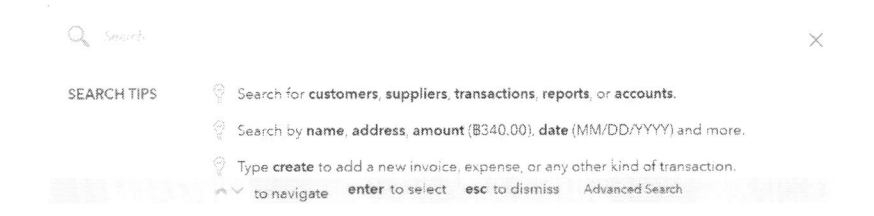

Notification bell – This bell button lets you view all notifications you receive from your QuickBooks activities and transactions.

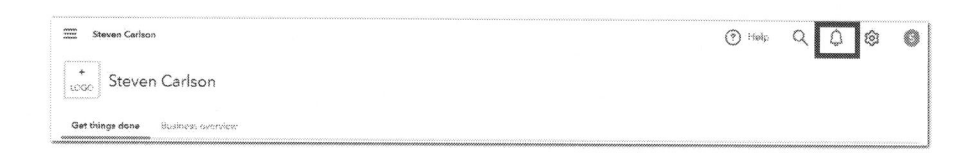

Settings or Gear icon – Manage your preference by using this icon.

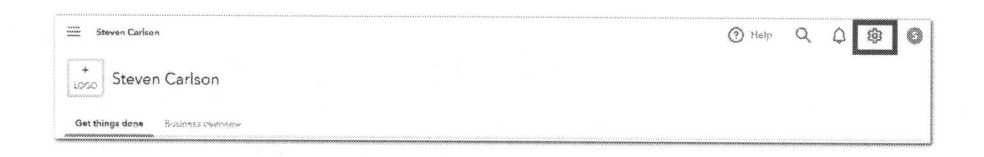

⊃ You can configure settings about your company, lists, tools, and profile.

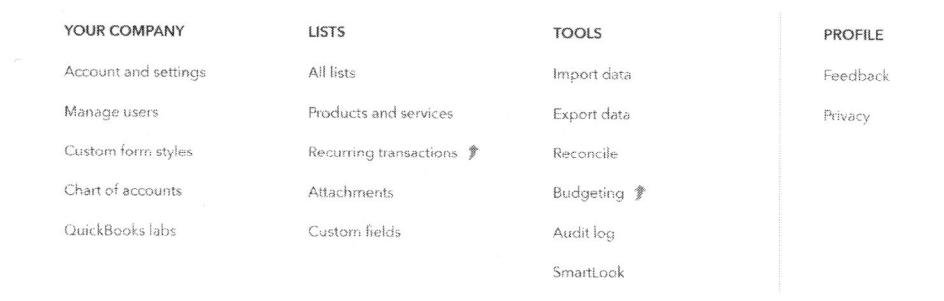

YOUR COMPANY	LISTS	TOOLS	PROFILE
Account and settings	All lists	Import data	Feedback
Manage users	Products and services	Export data	Privacy
Custom form styles	Recurring transactions	Reconcile	
Chart of accounts	Attachments	Budgeting	
QuickBooks labs	Custom fields	Audit log	
		SmartLook	

Account – At the top right corner is the button for you to sign out from your account. It also brings you to your Intuit account which gives you access across all Intuit products like QuickBooks through a single account.

Get Things Done

From the name itself, you can get many things done in this area of the dashboard. It displays shortcuts to several functions to your daily bookkeeping work, including:

- **Add customer** – Adds your customer information in just a few clicks so you can keep track of your invoices and manage customer data and analytics.
- **Add estimate** – Add estimates using this tab and send them to your customers automatically.
- **Add invoice** – Creates invoices instantly and lets you send it right away when you are done.
- **Receive payment** – Records receipt of payments from customers.
- **Write checks** – Makes check and adds details accordingly.
- **Print checks** – Print check instantly from wherever you are.

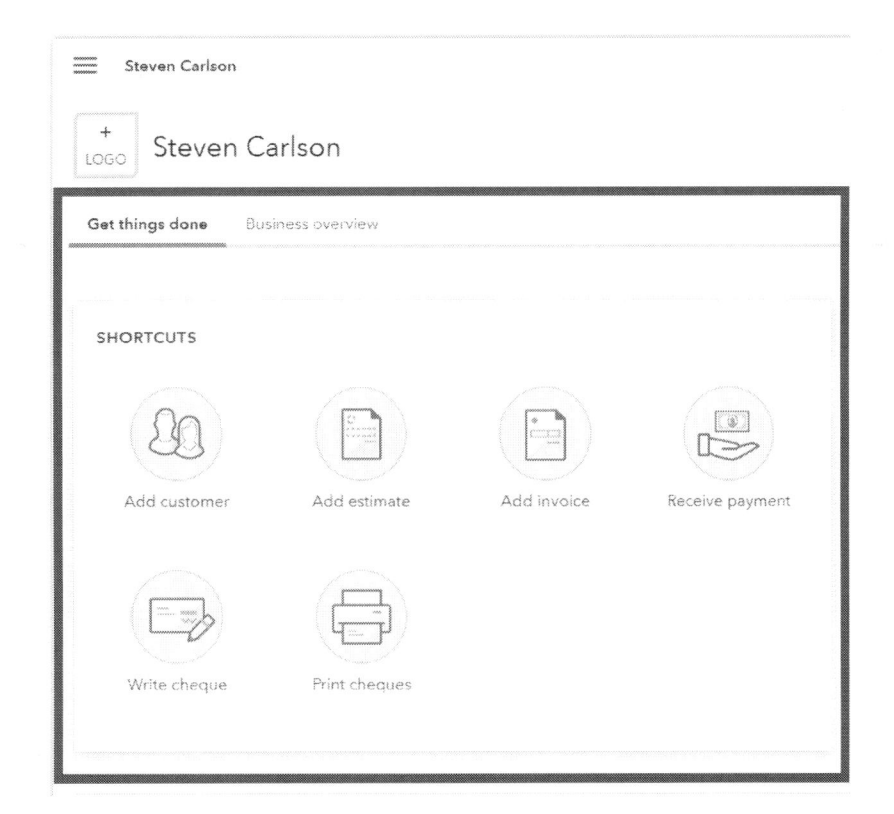

Business Overview

The Business Overview page in QuickBooks presents you with a quick report of your financial performance. You can easily view the status of your business, including your profit and loss, expenses, income, and sales on one screen.

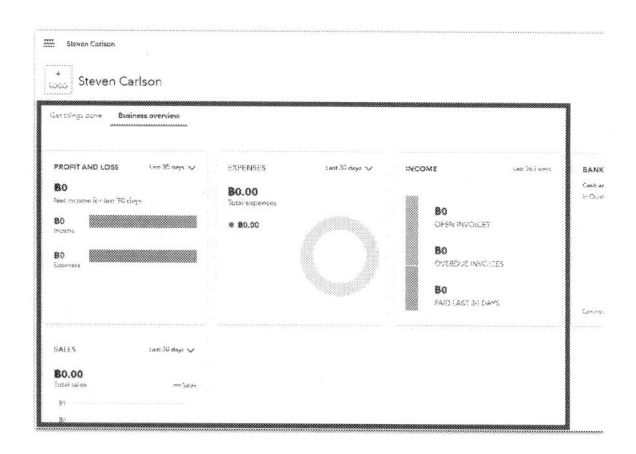

It is composed of smart charts and bars that you can click to show you comprehensive information. You can also select the duration of the report you want to view from the dropdown button.

This area of the dashboard screen is where you can observe and understand your cash flow from your bank account.

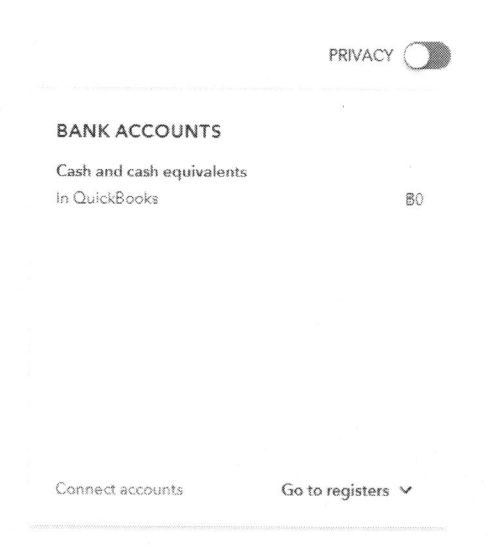

Other useful links in this panel include the ability to:

- **Connect accounts** – Connect your QuickBooks account to your financial accounts like banks.
- **Go to registers** – This link redirects you to Cash and Cash equivalents of your bank account history.
- **Privacy** – Turn on privacy to hide financial information on your dashboard.
- **See all activities** – Right below is the link to view all the past activities in your QuickBooks account.

Sidebar Menu

The sidebar menu or navigation bar on the left shows the key features of QuickBooks as well as your historical transactions.

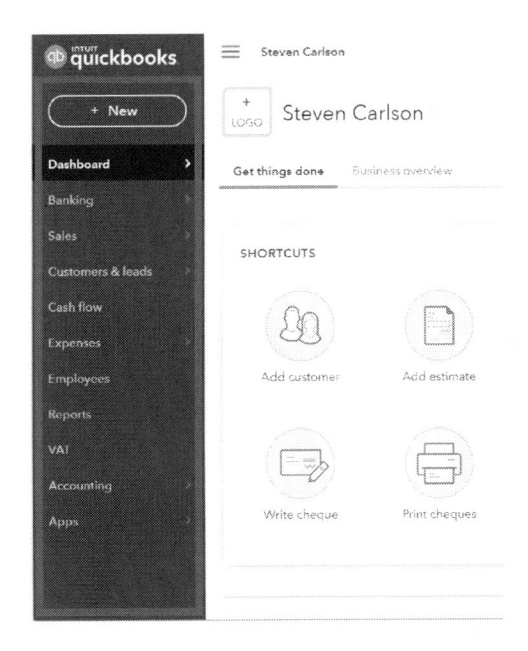

+ New – This tab shows you multiple actions you can choose for your customers, vendors, employees, and others.

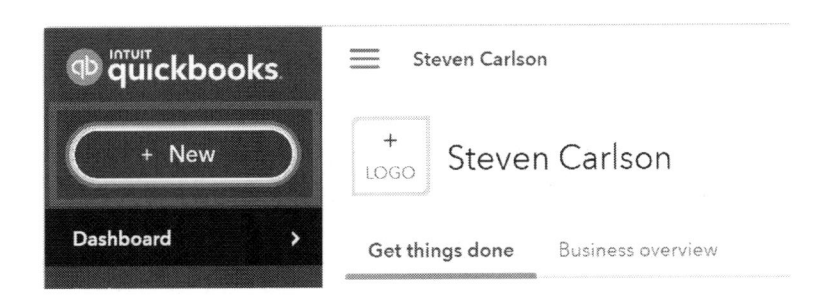

You can quickly run your day-to-day accounting tasks in just a few clicks with a variety of features and access available in this shortcut.

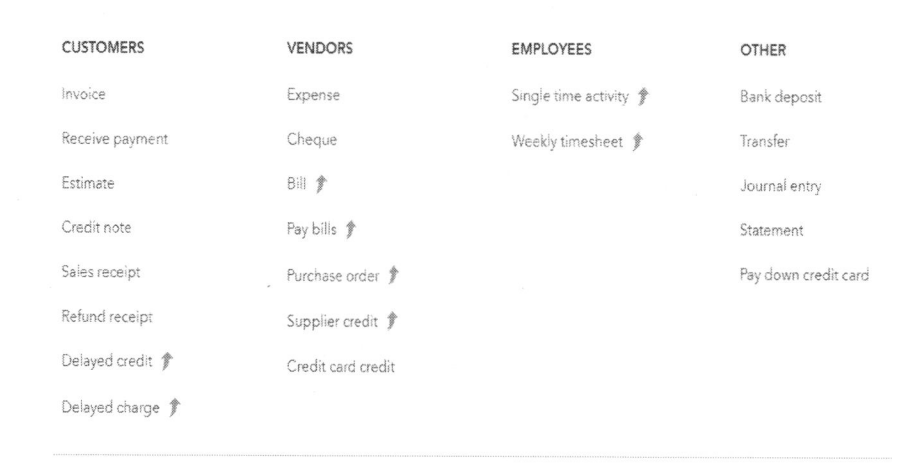

CUSTOMERS	VENDORS	EMPLOYEES	OTHER
Invoice	Expense	Single time activity	Bank deposit
Receive payment	Cheque	Weekly timesheet	Transfer
Estimate	Bill		Journal entry
Credit note	Pay bills		Statement
Sales receipt	Purchase order		Pay down credit card
Refund receipt	Supplier credit		
Delayed credit	Credit card credit		
Delayed charge			

Banking – Under the Banking menu we have the Banking and Rules tabs.

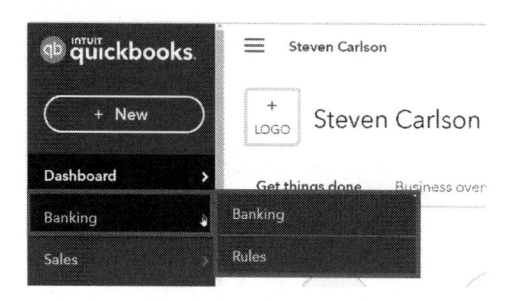

- **Banking** – Banking connects your bank accounts to your QuickBooks account so you can easily upload transactions and track your income and expenses.

- **Rules** – With Rules, you can set how you want to organize related bank records and transactions.

Sales – The Sales functionality is categorized into three tabs: All Sales, Customers, Products and Services.

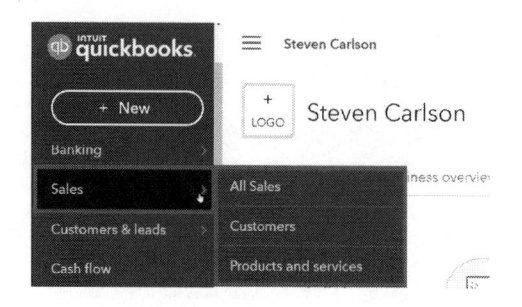

- **All Sales** – All Sales automates your invoicing by creating and tracking invoices. Additionally, you can customize your invoices to make them look more professional.
- **Customers** - You can view, manage, and add your customers' information on this page and keep track of your invoices.
- **Products and services** – This page is where your products and services are.

Customers and Leads – QuickBooks makes it simple for you to manage the most important thing in your business – keeping your customers and bringing in more leads.

- **Customers** – You can view, manage, and add your customers' information on this page while keeping track of your invoices.
- **Marketing** – The Marketing tab functions to support your efforts in customer retention and leads generation by personalizing messages and automating email marketing campaigns. QuickBooks connects to MailChimp so you can combine your contacts and reach out to customers efficiently.

Cash Flow – QuickBooks helps you track your cash flow. View your budget in detail and see how much you spend with a simple, real-time look at where your money is going.

Expenses – This feature easily tracks your business expenses all in one place. The Expenses menu is categorized as:

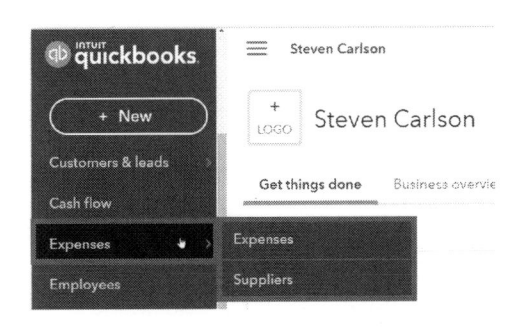

- **Expenses** – It records all your transactions and automates the tracking of bills, invoices, and payments which reduces your time spent on bookkeeping.
- **Suppliers** – This is where you can find the list of all your suppliers along with the summary of your bill status.

Employees – This menu is where you can manage all your employees or contractors.

Reports – Here you can run and manage your financial reports. There are tabs under this feature, namely the Standard, Custom reports, and Management reports.

- **Standard** – The Standard reports tab gives you basic accounting reports you need such as balance sheet, profit and loss, and cash flows.
- **Custom Reports** – This type of report enables you to customize reports to your liking.
- **Management Reports** - The Management reports are designed to create a professional report of your financial statements. Here you can select actions like edit, export, or print your report.

VAT – This is the menu where you can manage your tax via automated calculations and filing.

Accounting – The Accounting tab shows you advanced tools for bookkeeping and finance such as chart of accounts and bank reconciliation.

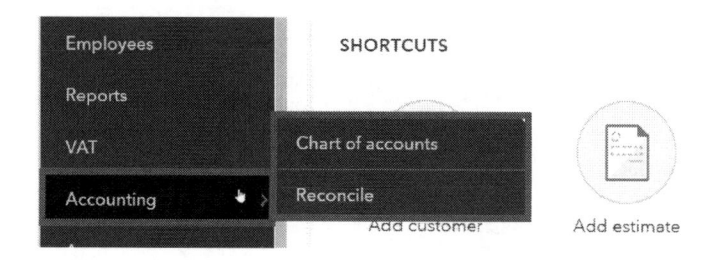

Chart of accounts – Chart of accounts is an index of your financial accounts of your business recorded on a ledger. This tab gives you an overview of a breakdown of your financial transactions.

Reconcile – All of your transactions between your bank accounts and QuickBooks are closely matched by reconciliation.

Apps – Under the Apps menu are Find Apps and My Apps:

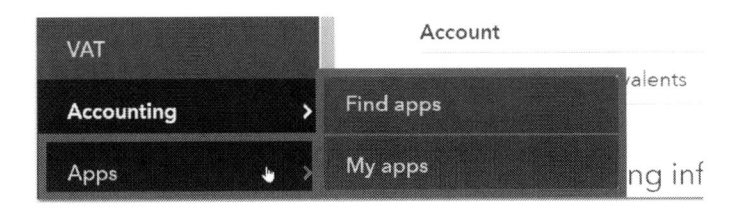

- **Find Apps** - Find Apps lets you connect your QuickBooks account to various apps that maximize your accounting and business experience.
- **My Apps** – In My Apps, you can view the apps that are connected to your QuickBooks.

HOW TO SET UP QUICKBOOKS FOR BUSINESS

As you move along this guide, the next step you need to do is to get your QuickBooks Online (QBO) account settled. This is one of the most important aspects of this tutorial, as you cannot proceed to run transactions successfully if you skip this part or if you lack knowledge in this area.

Setting up QuickBooks for your business is easy and simple. It is just like setting up any other program, such as social media, where you need to set up your personal profile. For starters, you'll need to enter some basic information about your company, followed by more accounting data. Once you have done that, you're ready to start using the software!

Add your Company Information

Customers want to know who is behind the products and services you sell, so it is important to tell them about your business. Your business information is automatically added to your invoices and other forms, so every time you send a form to your customers, they get to know your business better and build a relationship with them. It also lets you get more leads and spread the word about your brand.

1. On the upper right corner of your screen, click the **gear icon**.
2. Click **Account and Settings**.
3. You can also click the logo and company name at the top to add your company information.

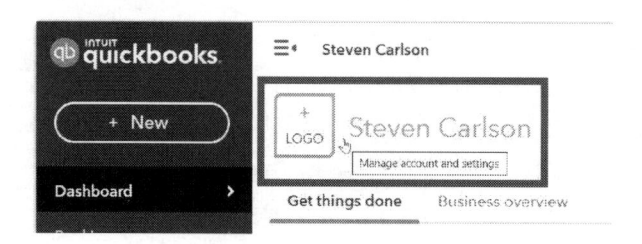

4. Under the **Company tab**, go to the company name and click the **pencil icon**.

5. To add your company logo, click the **plus button** in the box.

6. Click another **plus button** inside the box.

7. Select a logo from your device and click **Save**.

8. Enter your company name, UEN, and GST number, which secures proper tax treatment. Click **Save**.

Note: If you are a solo entrepreneur with no workers and no excise or pension tax returns, use your EIN as your business ID.

9. Fill out the rest of the fields under the **Company Type, Company Info**, and **Address**. Click the **pencil icon** and use **Save** on each tab when you add or edit information.

HOW TO ADD NEW CUSTOMERS

It's very important to have a list of customers in your accounting software so you can track and manage who needs to pay you.

1. From the sidebar menu, go to Customers and Leads tab and select **Customers**.

2. Click **New customer**.

3. Fill out the form with the following customer information:

- First name
- Last name
- Email
- Phone
- Mobile

You can also fill out the other fields with as many details as you want.

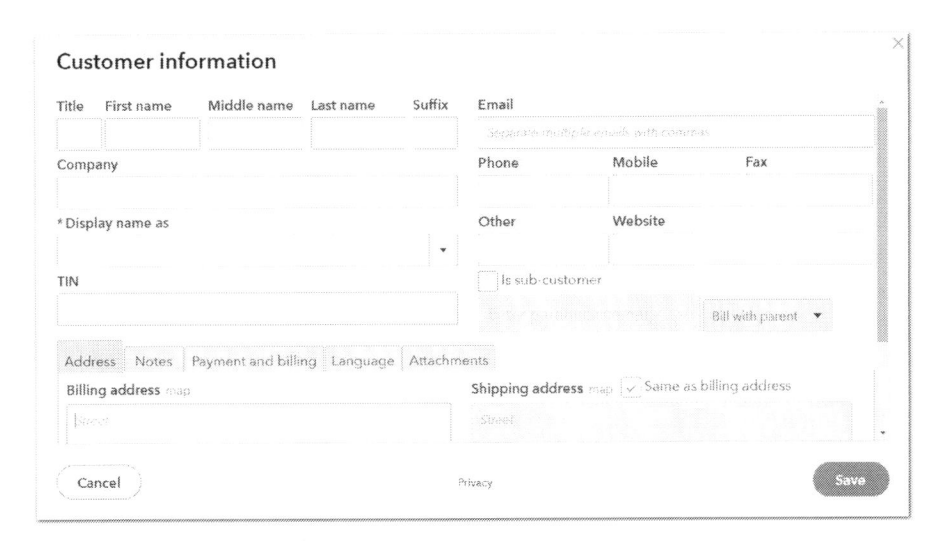

4. Tick the box next to **Is sub-customer** if this is a sub-customer. You can add a customer and make it as a parent or a sub-customer to organize your customer information better.

Then, click the **dropdown** and select a parent customer. Next, click the **dropdown** and select **bill with parent** or bill **this customer**.

If this is a parent customer, you can skip this field.

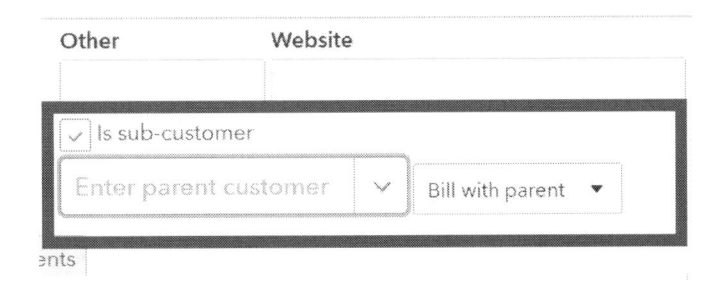

5. Enter the billing address. Tick the box if the shipping address is the same as the billing address.

6. You can also add information to the following tabs:

- **Notes** - Enter specific remarks for this customer if there are any you wish to add.
- **Payment and billing** - Select your payment and billing preference.

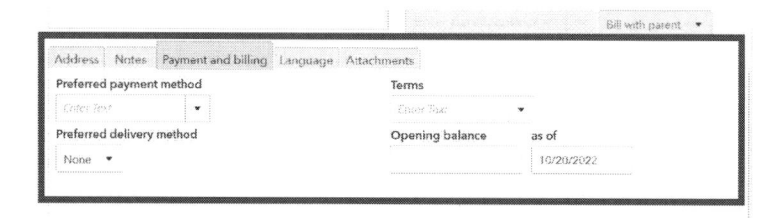

  - **Preferred payment method**: cash, credit card or debit card.
  - **Preferred delivery method**: Print later, Send later or none.
  - **Opening balance as of**: Enter amount and select the date from the calendar.
  - **Terms**: Due on receipt, Net 15, Net 30, or Net 60. You can also add a new term.
    1. Click the **dropdown** and select **Add new**.
    2. Add a name to your new term.
    3. Select your preferred due days then, enter the number of days. Click **Save**.

- **Language** - Choose the language you want your invoice to be sent in. Click the **dropdown** and select a language from the list.

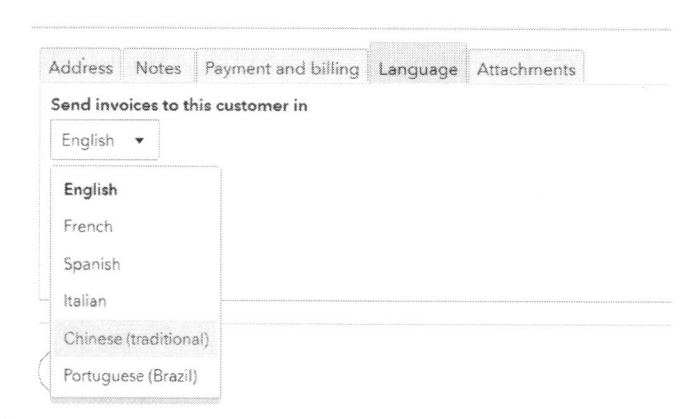

- **Attachments** - Upload attachments with a minimum size of 20mb. Drag and drop files in the box or click the attachments icon.

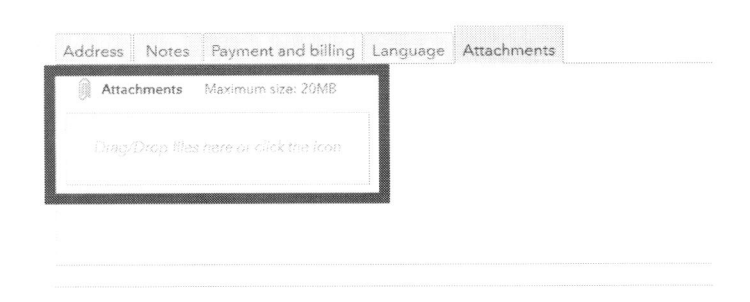

7. Once you are satisfied with the information you entered, click **Save**.

8. If you want to edit the information later after adding a customer, simply click the name of the customer on the customer page.

9. Click **Edit** then **Save** when you're done editing.

HOW TO ADD NEW PRODUCTS AND SERVICES

To run a business well, you need to be able to keep track of the things you purchase from your suppliers and how you bring them all together in your storage space and ready for distribution. QuickBooks Online makes it easy and quick to set up the products and services that you buy and sell.

Once your items are in the system, they are automatically kept track of and added to any transactions you are working on. This automation helps you plan for the future and keep track of your budget, which are both important for your growing business.

1. Go to the **Sales** menu and click **Products and Services**.

2. Click **Add a product or service**.

3. You are prompted to select between **Non-inventory** or **Services**.

Note: The product or service you buy and/or sell is divided into two types: **Non-inventory and Service**.

Non-inventory products are those you buy and/or sell but don't track quantities of such as installation nuts and bolts. **Service** refers to the things you do for your customers, like landscaping or helping them with their taxes.

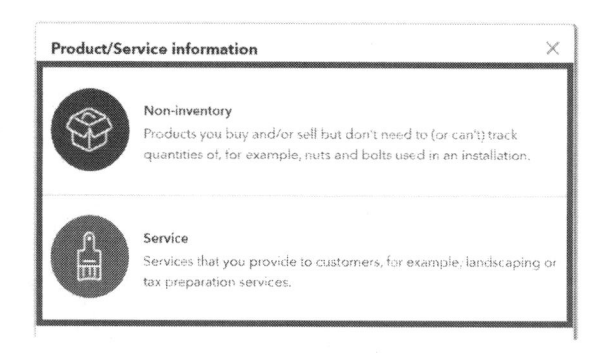

4. Enter the **Name** of your product. If you want to track your product, add **SKU**.

5. Click the **pencil icon** to upload a picture of your product for easy tracking, if available.

6. Select a category. To add a new category, click the drop down and click **Add New**.

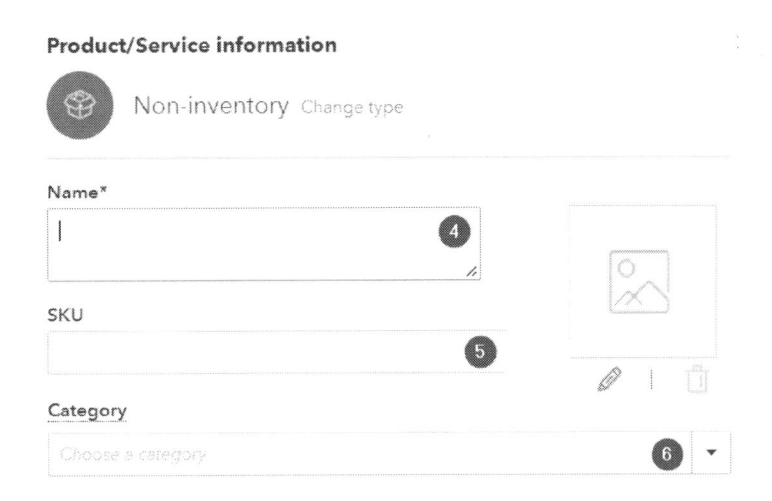

7. Enter a name for your category. Click **Save**.

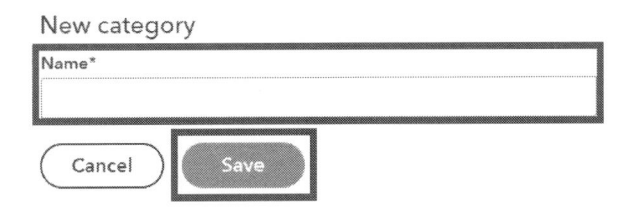

8. Add your product **Description**, which will appear on your sales form every time you create a transaction.

9. Add the **Sales price**. Click the **dropdown** to select an **Income account** you want to link for this item. QuickBooks has a default Sales Income you can select among the list of other income accounts.

10. You can click **Save and close** but if you want to add a new product, click the **dropdown**, and click **Save and new**.

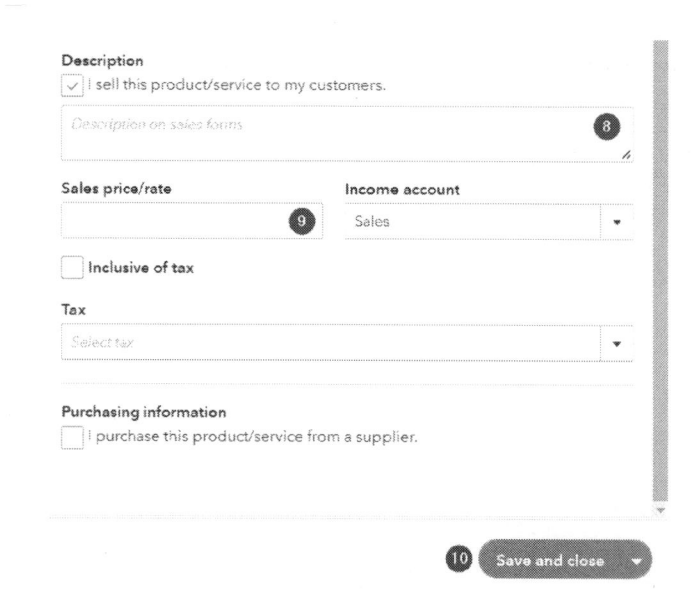

Now you have your new product listed on the Products and Services page.

Alternatively, you can add your products and services through the gear icon.

1. Click the **gear icon** on the header.
2. Select **Products and Services** under the Lists section to redirect you to the Products and Services page. Start adding your items following the same instructions as above.

HOW TO SET UP CHART OF ACCOUNTS

In the beginning of this chapter, you learned how to navigate to the Chart of Accounts tab in QuickBooks. Now, you will learn how to set up the Chart of Accounts to record all your financial transactions correctly and keep better track of your overall business performance.

Chart of Accounts (COA) is one of the most important parts of the accounting system, so knowing how to set up a Chart of Accounts in QuickBooks is important. It serves as an accurate financial report that shows a list and numbers of the money coming in your business, expenses, debts, and others. Everything that comprises your business is stated in the Chart of Accounts and is organized with proper labels and details. Missing items or errors in accounts are easily tracked and identified with the help of the COA.

There are two different financial statements that are part of the COA, **the balance sheet**, and **the income statement**.

Balance sheet - The balance sheet gives you a view of what your business owns, how much it owes, and how much it is worth. This lets you know how your business is doing financially right now. The three types of accounts that make up the balance sheet are:

A. **Asset account** - Asset accounts report any resource of your business that are valuable to the business, including:

- Land
- Buildings
- Equipment
- Vehicles

B. **Liability accounts** - This one refers to the records for all the debts your business owes, including:

- Bills
- Bank loans
- Credit card loans
- Mortgage

C. **Equity accounts** - Equity accounts record what you get after you deduct liability accounts from its assets. Simply put, Assets - Liabilities = Equity. It also measures how valuable your business is. Below are some samples of equities:

- Common stocks
- Dividends
- Preferred stocks

Income statement - This financial statement shows your business' earnings over a period of time by subtracting your expenses from your income.

D. **Revenue accounts** - This account type registers the income your business makes by selling products or providing services, such as:

- Sales income
- Service revenue
- Rental income
- Investment

Revenue accounts give you a clear picture of your income, and sorting this type of account by source is a better way to know which area of your business generates the most cash.

E. **Expense Account** - Your expense account contains all of the money that you have spent generating income. If you are renting a space, for example, the payment is designated for your rent expenses. You will be able to keep track of the movement of your money from cash to expense accounts.

- Salaries
- Rent
- Cost of sales
- Marketing expense

As you set up your Chart of Accounts, you have to put your accounts into one of these two groups.

1. Go to the **Accounting** menu and select the **Chart of Accounts**.
2. Click **New**.
3. Create an account set up with the following fields:

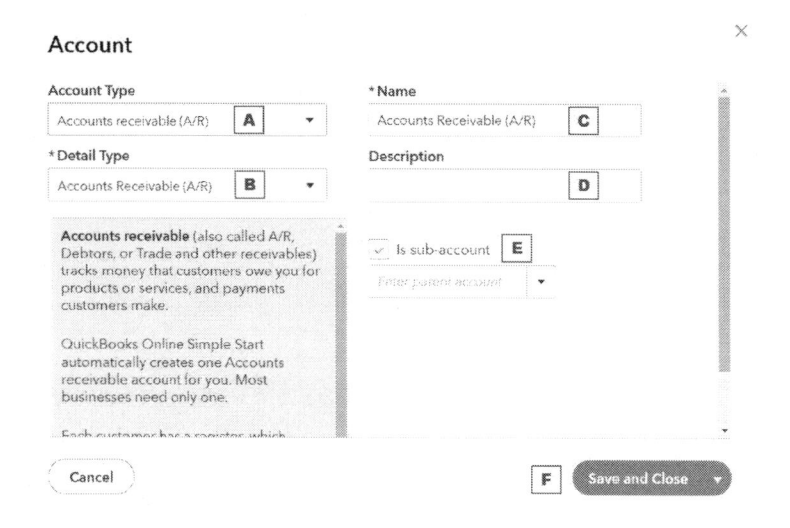

A. **Account Type** - Select an account from the **dropdown**.
B. **Detail Type** - Click the **dropdown** and select a detail type for your account. There is a help guide in the grey box below that you can refer to selecting a detail type.
C. **Name** - Clear the default name on this field and enter a name that's easier to identify in your transactions.
D. **Description** - This field may be optional.
E. **Is sub-account** - You can create an account and make it a parent or sub-account to organize your accounts better. Tick the box next to "Is sub-account" if this is a sub-account. Next, click the **dropdown** to select its parent account.

F.   Click **Save and Close**. If you want to create another account, click the **dropdown**, and select **Save and New**. Your new account is now added to the chart of accounts.

You can also click the **gear icon** on the header, then click the Chart of Accounts under your company.

IMPORTING SPREADSHEETS AND DESKTOP DATA

Bringing your data into QuickBooks saves you time when entering the most important information into your account. Instead of recording this one by one, you can easily import files that already have lists and details you want in your database.

To import data successfully, you need to make sure that QuickBooks can read your file. On the upload page, you can find a link to a sample Excel spreadsheet that will help you follow the correct format. Most imports accept CSV files or Excel worksheets.

You've already learned how to manually add new **Customers**, **Products and Services**, and **Chart of Accounts**. In this section, you'll find out how to add all of the data in one go. Importing a file applies to **Bank Data, Customers, Suppliers, Chart of Accounts, Products and Services, Invoices**, and **Bills** and except for the "Bank Data" import, the process is the same for most imports, so that you can follow the same steps.

1.   Click the **gear icon** on the upper right of the screen.

2.   Select **Import data** under the Tools section.

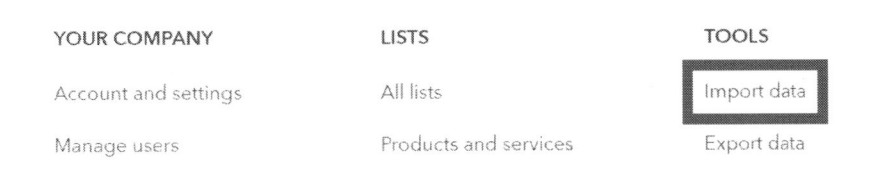

3.   Click the type of data you want to import.

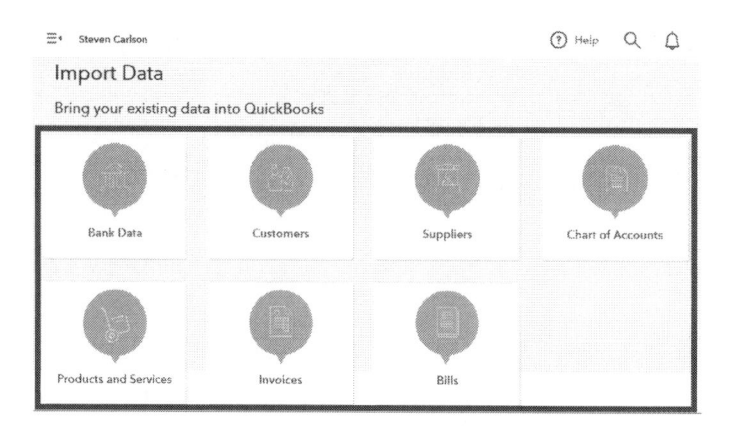

4. Click **Browse** and look for the file you want to import.

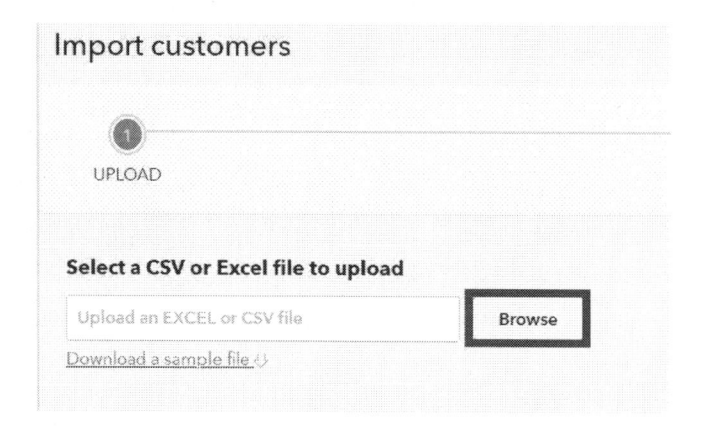

5. After choosing your file, click **Next**.

6. Map your spreadsheet to QuickBooks fields. Click the **dropdown** arrow and select one of the columns in your Excel file to match the column's contents into QuickBooks. Click **Next**.

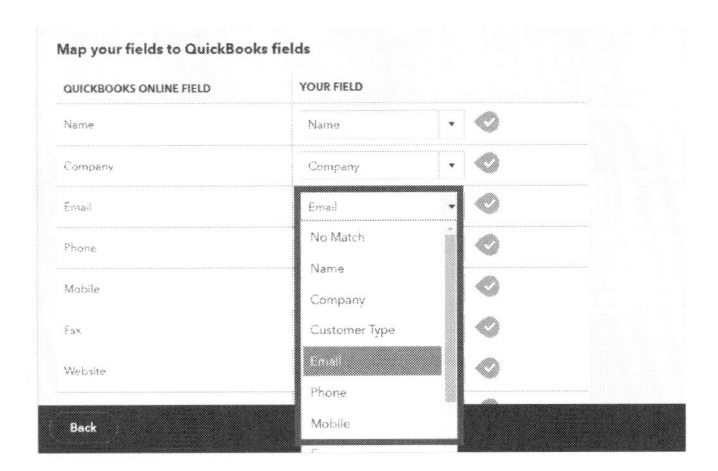

7. The import page shows the list of customers ready to be imported. You can manage this data using the filter bar, edit into the cell or untick boxes to leave out columns you don't need.

8. Click **Import** once you are satisfied with your data.

9. You will be able to view the data imported on the same page when you manually record this type of information.

03
ACCOUNTING

Whether you are a small business owner or part of a larger organization, QuickBooks Online is the fastest way to stay on top of your finances and grow your financial security. In this chapter, you'll learn the basics of QBO's banking feature, which lets you easily connect your bank and credit card accounts and see what's coming in and going out. You can take advantage of this "Bank Feed" feature and track your bank transactions on a daily basis.

Bank Feeds has the ability to let you review each transaction, categorize it into the right account, add it to QuickBooks, and omit it if you don't need it in your records. On top of that, you can transfer funds and split transactions to make your banking experience more efficient.

You can reconcile your bank accounts in QuickBooks Online. This is an important part of accounting because it shows a current financial overview of your business. Bank reconciliation is something you can learn more about as you go along.

Working with an accountant gives you expert advice to help you with any issues with your financial records, and QuickBooks makes it easy for you to collaborate. At the end of this chapter, we'll talk about how to give your accountant access to your account.

HOW TO CONNECT A BANK ACCOUNT OR CREDIT CARD

When you link your bank and credit card accounts to QuickBooks, it pulls data directly from your bank automatically. This saves you time because you do not have to add each bank transaction by hand to keep track of your money from your everyday business dealings. That is how the Bank Feeds work for you. With this feature, you can link your account to multiple banks and upload historical data. You can even choose how far back you want to import data from.

Adding transactions from your bank and credit card accounts can be done in two ways. One way is to link your bank account to QuickBooks so that your transactions can be downloaded automatically. The other way is to get a file of your business's past transactions from your bank and credit card, then upload it to your account to import those transactions. If you cannot get your bank to connect to your account, you should do the manual process.

Connect your Bank to your Account

1. Go to **Banking** from the **Banking** menu.
2. Click **Connect account**.

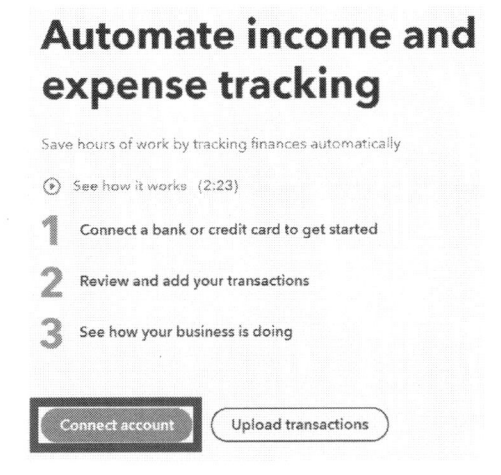

3. From the list of banking institutions, select your bank or credit card. You can also type in the name of your bank or credit card company and choose it from the list.

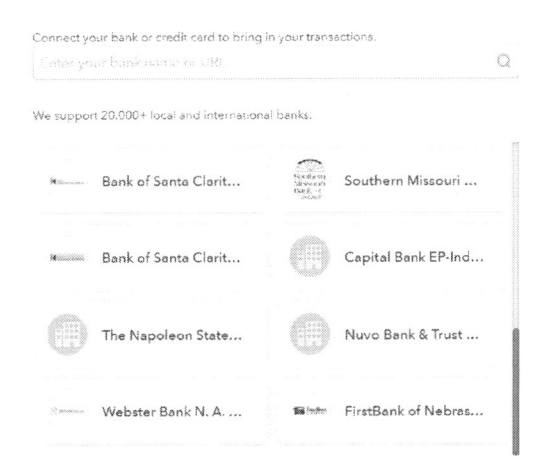

4. Enter the **username** and **password** you use to log into your bank or credit card's online banking, then click **Continue**.

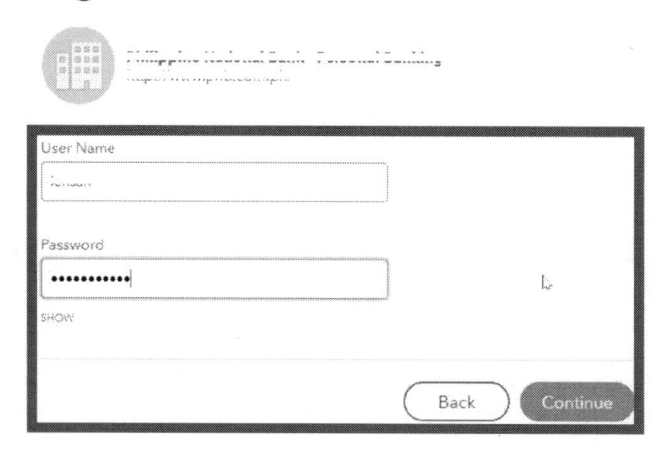

5. Depending on your bank and credit card, you may have to take a few more steps to comply with security features. Complete these steps. Click **Continue** to move forward.

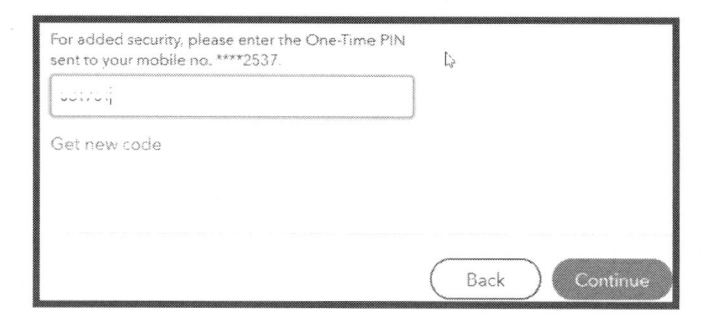

6. When you're done with the steps to sign in, QuickBooks looks for all the accounts you have in your bank. Link your account to the available account types.

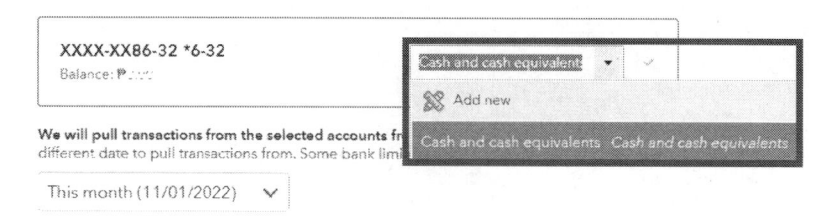

7. QuickBooks lets you import from the beginning of the business year, but you can choose how far back you want to download transactions. Click the dropdown and select which period you want. Click **Connect** when you're done.

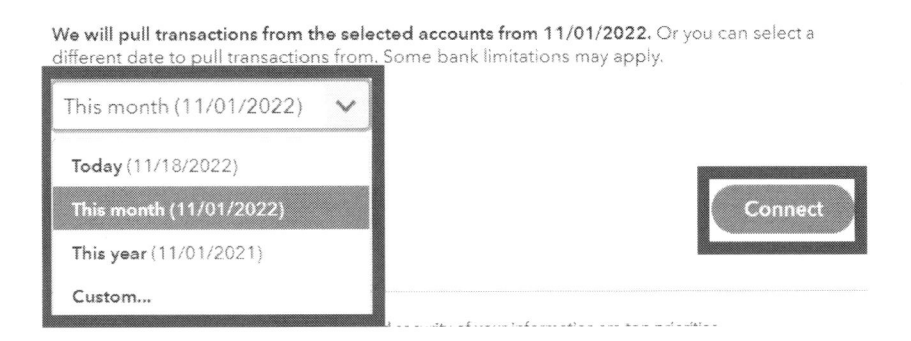

8. Once the connection is successful, you can now view your bank or credit card transactions from the time the data was pulled up and going forward.

As mentioned earlier, there is an option to manually import your transactions like bank statements if your bank does not support QuickBooks.

Manually Upload your Transactions

1. Click the **gear icon** on the header.
2. Select **Import data** under the Tools section.
3. Click **Bank Data**.

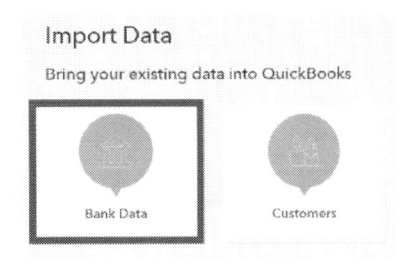

4. Log in to your online bank account and export your bank statement in a CSV, QFX, QBO, OFX, or TXT format.
5. Upload your bank statement. Drag and drop files into the box or click the upload box and select a file from your device.

6. Click **Continue**.

7. Select which QuickBooks account you want to assign to those transactions that you uploaded, then click **Continue**

8. Set up your file by answering questions about the format of your data.

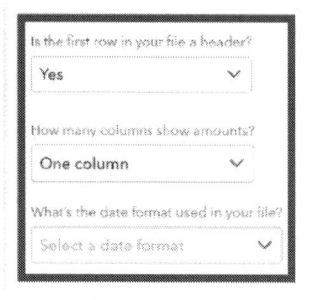

9. Select the fields that correspond to your file. Click **Continue**.

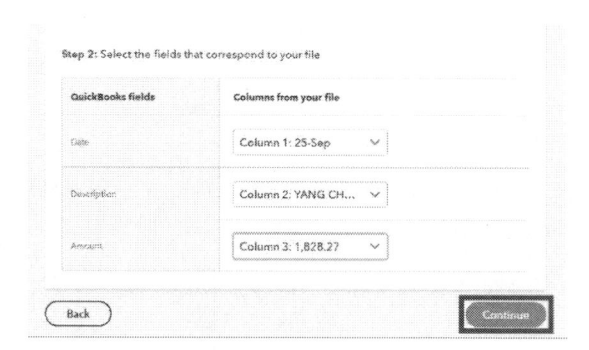

10. Tick the boxes of the transactions you want to include in the upload. Click **Continue**.

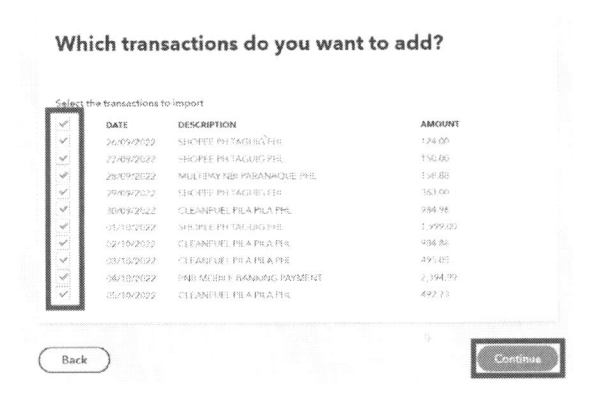

11. A window will appear confirming the import you want to make. Click **Yes** to confirm.
12. Another window will pop up to inform you of the import status and the next step. Once you understand this, click **Done**.

UNDERSTANDING THE BANK FEEDS

Once you have successfully connected your bank account, you can now see what transactions you've recently made. To get the most out of online banking, it is important to understand how bank feeds work. Bank feeds can show you how much money comes in, keep track of your expenses, and give you insights into your up-to-date cash flow.

So, the next steps for your bank feeds are to review each transaction, categorize it in the right account on your chart of accounts, and then add it to QuickBooks. This feature also includes a number of other helpful services, all of which will contribute to the increased productivity of your banking and accounting operations. This is what your banking page looks like after connecting your bank and credit cards to QuickBooks. Let us start with the steps on how to manage your bank feeds.

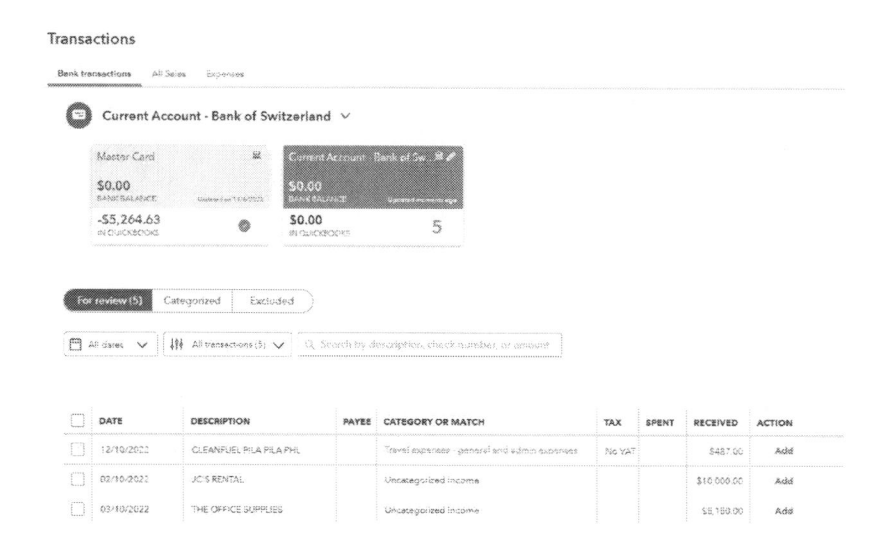

1. On the top section of your online banking page, you can see bank and credit card accounts set up. You can switch between accounts by clicking the **dropdown** to select an account whose transactions you want to see.

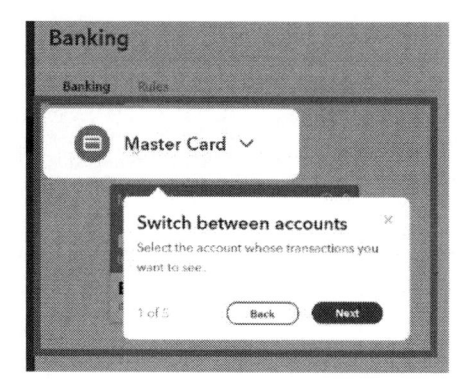

2. Scroll down to see your bank transactions under the **For review**. This tab lets you review information such as payee and category and amount of each transaction so you can check if it contains the correct details.

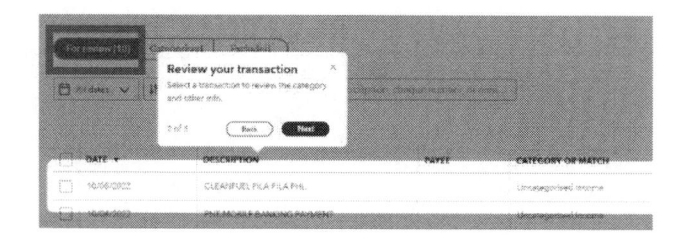

3. To view more information, click transaction. You can make any changes or add any details you want, including the following:

A. Categorize

B. Find match

C. Record as transfer

D. Record as credit card payment

A. **Categorize**

Choose a category to keep your books in order. Over time, QuickBooks understands how you want to organize your transactions and makes online banking easier by suggesting categories based on what you have done in the past.

1. Click the **dropdown** to select a payee. This indicates the name of a supplier or customer that you will be able to see when you later run a report.

2. Click the **dropdown** to select a category your transaction belongs to.

3. Add or edit notes.

4. You have options to **add attachments, create a rule** that you can use to frequently occur transactions or **exclude** a transaction to leave it out from the list.

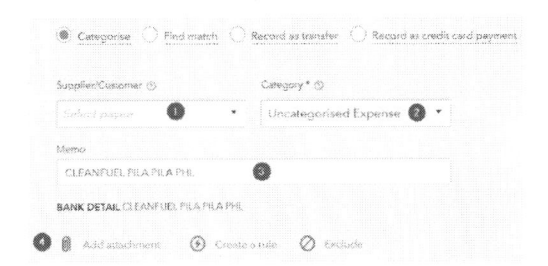

5. Click **Add** once you are satisfied with the details.

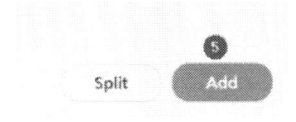

B. **Find Match**

To avoid duplicate entries, match a transaction to an existing record.

1. Click **Find Match**. A match window pops up to help you look for any transaction that might match with an existing record.
2. Use the filters to help you find a transaction. Click the magnifying glass to search items.

3. Click the checkbox to the left of the item you are looking for.
4. Click **Save** when you're happy with the match. You can locate the matched transaction under "Matched" in the "All transactions" tab.

C. **Record as Transfer**

Use the Record as transfer tab when your transaction moves money from one account of the same bank to another account of the same bank.

1. Click **Record as transfer**.
2. Click the **dropdown** and select an account.

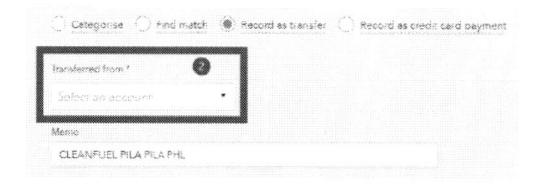

3. Click **Add.**

D. **Record as Credit Card Payment**

Record as credit card payment registers a bank transaction done via credit card payment.

1. Click the **dropdown** and select a credit card payment source.

2. Click the **dropdown** to select a supplier.

3. Click **Add**.

4. You can also **Add** a transaction to your books even without opening it.

5. You can still make changes after adding a transaction. Click the **Categorized** tab to edit.

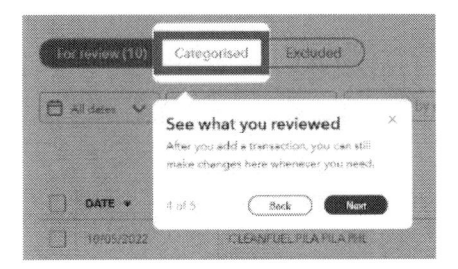

6. Click the account under the Added or Matched section.

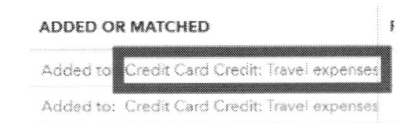

7. Manage a transaction you just categorized by editing some details in this window. You can make changes with the payee, bank/credit card as well as the category. Click **Save and close**.

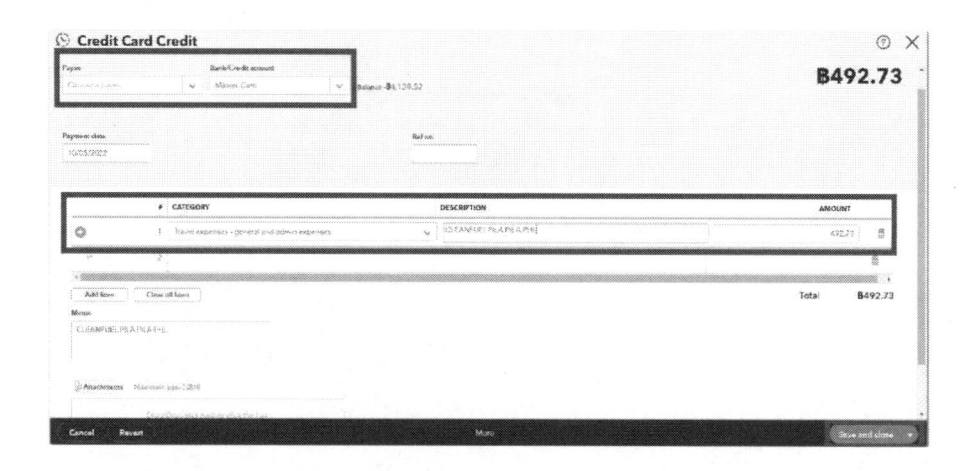

8. Personal or duplicated transactions tagged excluded are moved to the **Excluded** tab. You can change this action by clicking **Undo**.

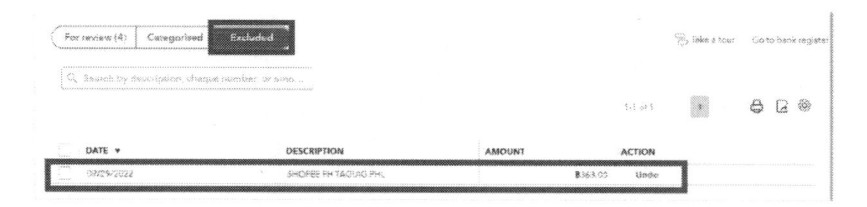

Bank feeds offer other services to make your online banking more efficient, such as creating rules and split transactions.

CREATE A RULE AND SPLIT TRANSACTIONS

Create a Rule

You can create rules to speed up the review process and automate categorizing your transactions. After setting up these rules, QuickBooks identifies your way of categorizing items and copies other information you entered in the past to save you time in organizing your books.

1. Go to the **Banking** menu and select **Rules**.

2. Click **New rule**.

3. On the create a rule window, fill out the following:

A. Enter a name for your new rule.

B. Select where you want to apply the transactions and bank account.

C. Choose your preferred conditions on how you want to trigger this rule. Use the conditions fields to apply rules according to the **Description**, **Bank text**, or **Amount**. Set the remaining formats to complete your conditions.

D. Click the **+Add a condition** to create more conditions.

E. Test the rule to see if the conditions are met and if you need to make any changes.

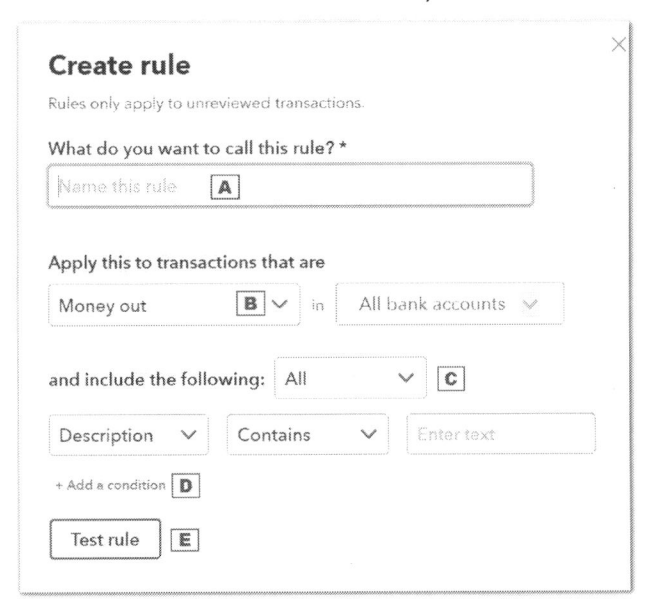

F. Select **Assign** if you want to further set up your rule, otherwise select **Exclude.** Choose the **Transaction type, Category,** and **Payee**.

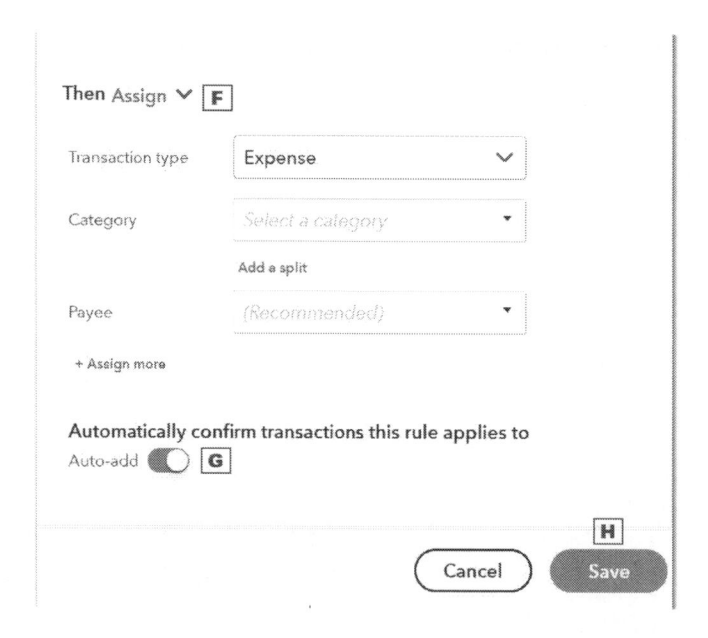

G. Toggle **Auto-add** to automatically confirm transactions that this rule applies to.

H. Select **Save**.

Split Transactions

When you're categorizing a single transaction, you have the option to split them into multiple categories. You can split transactions between business, amount, and etc.

1. On the Banking page, click on a transaction you want to split. Under the Categorize tab, click **Split.**

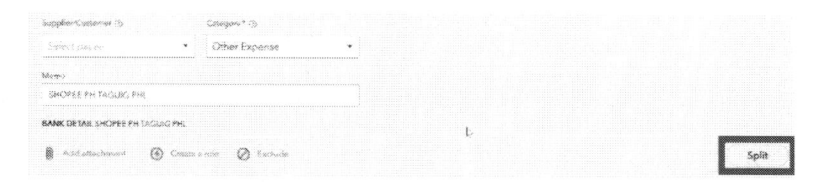

2. Fill out the split transaction form.

    A. Select a payee, if applicable.

    B. Enter your first **Category**, **Description** and **Amount**.

    C. Add the second item on the next line

    D. If you need more lines, click **Add line**. Click **Reset** to clear items.

E. Make sure the total is the same as the transaction amount. Below the lines, you can check the split amount, original amount, and the difference.

F. After you split the transaction successfully, click **Apply and accept**.

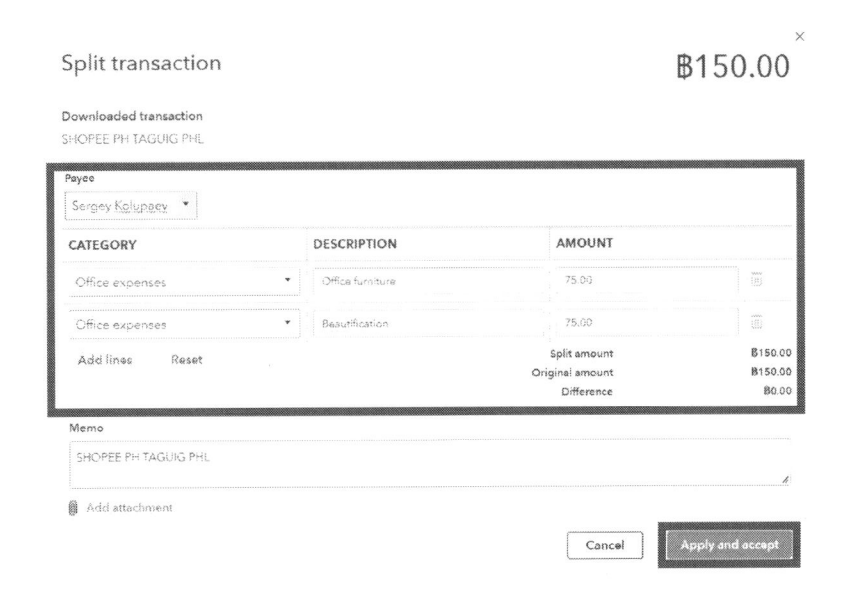

RECONCILING AN ACCOUNT. WHAT IT IS FOR AND HOW DO YOU DO IT

Bank reconciliation is the process of matching a company's cash balance in an accounting record with the business transactions declared on the bank statements. Reconciling your bank accounts helps compare records and identify any differences between the two so you can make sure that your business' financial report is correct. It also helps minimize human errors and prevents causing risks.

You can reconcile your bank and credit card accounts in QuickBooks and compare them with the corresponding transactions on your bank statements. QuickBooks automates bank reconciliation by connecting with the bank feed, so you can save time and receive accurate results. It is recommended to complete bank reconciliations regularly to keep your cash records up to data and accurate.

Reconcile Accounts via Bank Feeds

1. Click the **Accounting** menu then click **Reconcile**.
2. Select the account you want to reconcile.

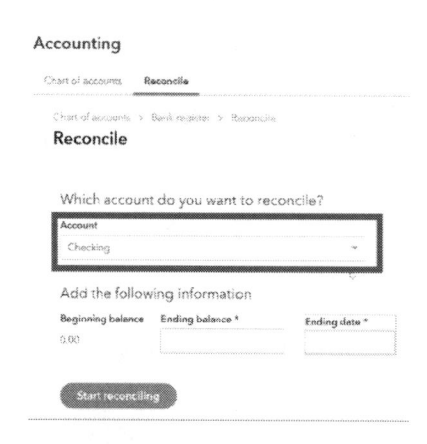

3. Enter the **Ending balance** and **Ending date** which comes from your bank or credit card statement.

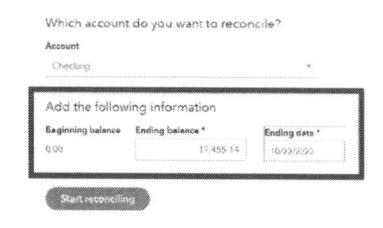

4. Click **Start reconciling**.

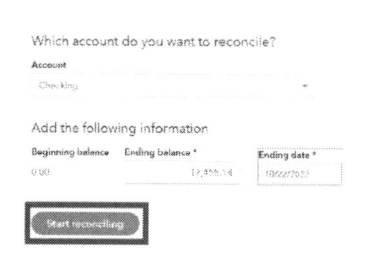

5. The next screen shows your account reconciliation activity with some key information to take note of. As displayed on the top, the "Cleared Balance" is subtracted from the "Statement Ending Balance" to get the "Difference." In the process of reconciling, the difference between the two numbers should be $0 which means your QuickBooks transactions and bank statements are balanced.

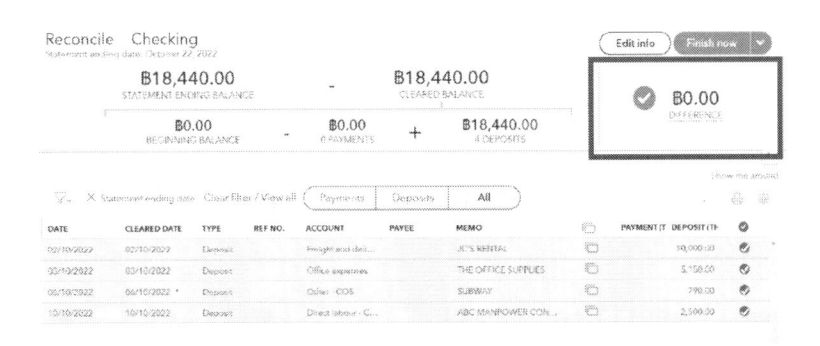

6. QuickBooks shows all transactions before the Statement end date. To change the display, use the filters on the filter pane to narrow down the list of transactions. Moreover, click the **Payments**, **Deposits** and **All** tabs to view transactions the same way.

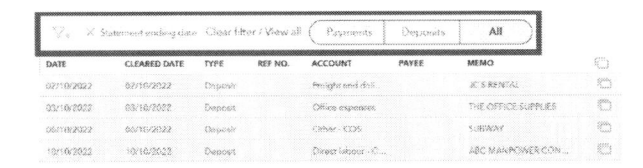

7. Add or remove a tick to select transactions you want to include in this reconciliation. QuickBooks will update the Difference as you do this.

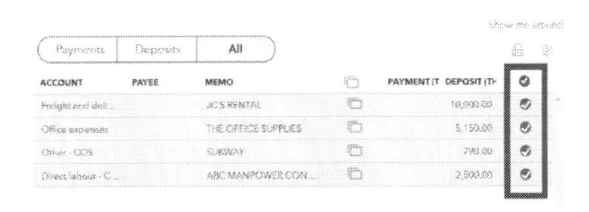

8. If your difference isn't getting to ฿0.00 and you think the information you entered isn't correct, select **Edit info** to make changes.

9. Edit the information then click **Save**.

10. You can click **Finish now** to end the reconciliation. Click the **dropdown** to select other options

if you are still not finished.

11. Click **Done** to complete the reconciliation.
12. To view a report of this reconciliation, go to the Reconcile tab under the Accounting menu and click **Summary** or **History by account**.

History by account shows you the reconciliation report with the total amount of deposits, credits, checks, and payments that have been cleared since the last reconciliation while the Summary shows you reconciliation summary. Click on each item listed to view its corresponding reconciliation report.

Note: Alternatively, you can click the **gear icon** on the header and select Reconcile under Tools to begin the bank reconciliation.

HOW TO INVITE AN ACCOUNTANT TO VIEW YOUR ACCOUNT

Accountants are specialists who manage a company's financial records by recording, verifying, and analyzing financial transactions. It's always a great idea to turn to Certified Professional Accountants if ever you find yourself in need of some help or advice about your business' financial matters.

The good thing is that QuickBooks makes it easier and faster to work with an accountant. Invite your accountant to view your account to check your books, make any necessary adjustments, and work with you to solve any problems that may arise.

You can add up to two accountants in QuickBooks Online Simple Start, Essentials, and Plus, while the Advance plan allows you to add up to three. Invite your accountant to QuickBooks Online by following these steps:

1. Click the **gear icon** on the upper right of the screen.
2. Click **Manage users**.
3. Click **Add User**.

4. The Select user type window has an indication of selected Company admin by default. This means that by adding this user, they will be able to view and create actions exactly like an admin. Click **Next**.

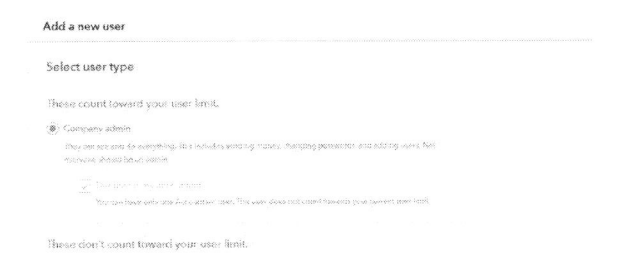

5. Enter the following contact details and Click **Save**

- First name
- Last name
- Email (for the user id)

6. Upon saving the information, the email invite to view your account is also sent to your accountant's email address. The accountant's details registers in the users list of your account.

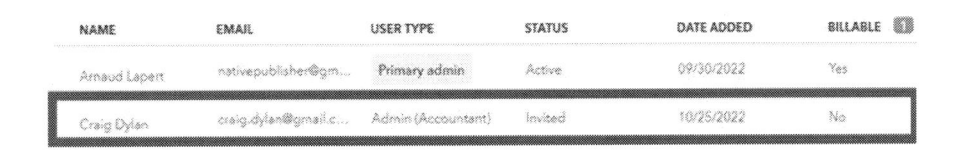

7. Your Accountant should click on the sign-in invitation link from the email sent to view and access your QuickBooks account.

8. If your accountant does not receive the invitation link, you can ask them to check the invitation in the spam folder. Or it may happen that you have entered the email address incorrectly for the details of the accountant. If both points are correct, you can check on your accountant's server that could be blocking the email.

9. If nothing works, you can resend the invitation to your accountant. Click the **gear icon** and then click **Manage users**. Select the accountant that you want to invite again by clicking **Resend invite** in the action column.

| Admin (Accountant) | Invited | 10/25/2022 | No | Resend invite ▼ |

04
EXPENSES

One of the best things about using QuickBooks is that it can easily track your business expenses – all in one place. QuickBooks records all your transactions as you would in paper and automates the tracking of bills, invoices, and payments which lessens your time on bookkeeping and allows you more time in running your business.

QuickBooks categorizes your expenses and helps you stay on top of your tax obligations. It also keeps track of sales tax right out of the box. Moreover, it provides you with reports on your income and expenses, helping you manage cash flow and achieve your financial goals. This will allow you to see exactly where your money is going and help you keep a careful eye on your finances and budget.

HOW TO ADD NEW SUPPLIERS

A supplier is a person or entity who delivers the goods and services to your business needs and is considered a part of your expenses. Adding suppliers to QuickBooks automates your billing information and gives you an organized record.

1. From the sidebar menu, go to **Expenses** and click **Suppliers**.
2. Click New **Supplier** on the top right.

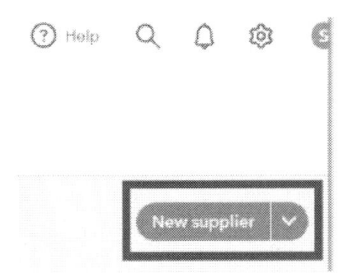

3. Fill out the form with the information you need.

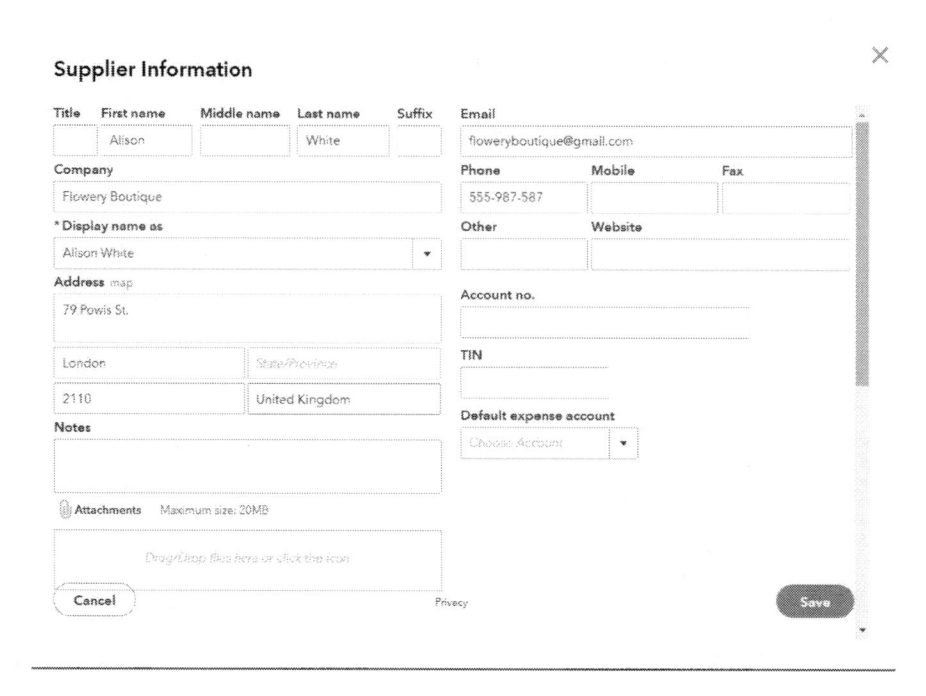

You can also add attachments and select a default expense account or add a new one.

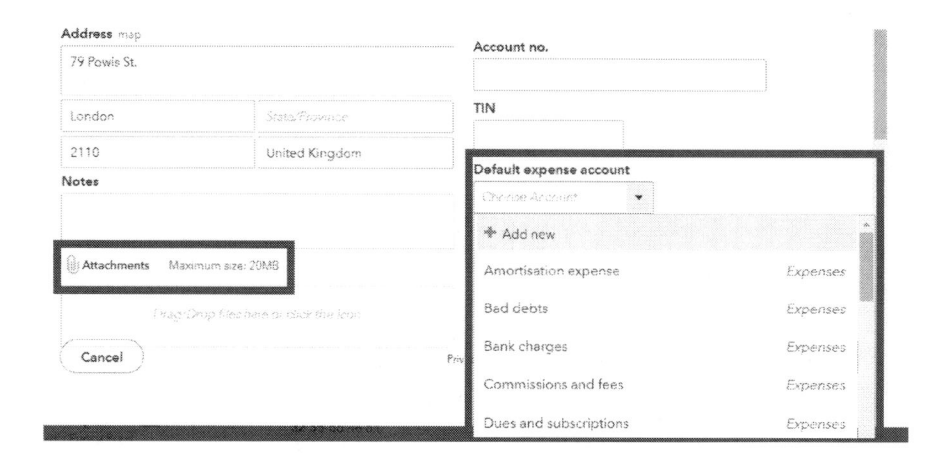

4. When you are done with the form, click Save. The new supplier is now added to the list.

Note: Alternatively, you can import a file of a list of customers. Read about how to import a file here.

HOW TO ADD EXPENSES AND WHAT ARE THE TYPES OF EXPENSES

QuickBooks Online makes it simple to document expenses. With both income and expenses in your bookkeeping, you can get a more accurate view of your business's financial health.

Expenses are for immediate payment of goods and services, as opposed to bills, which are for later payment. Use Expense if the expense has already been paid for or if payment is due immediately.

1. Select **+ New** from the side navigation bar.
2. Click the **Expense** tab under the Vendors section.
3. Select the vendor in the **Payee** field. This helps keep tabs on your expenses and the people you're paying.

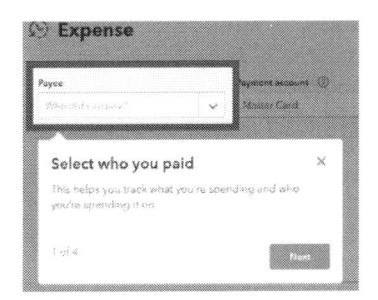

4. Select the account you used to pay for the expense in the **Payment account** field. This shows the source of the funds used to pay this expense.

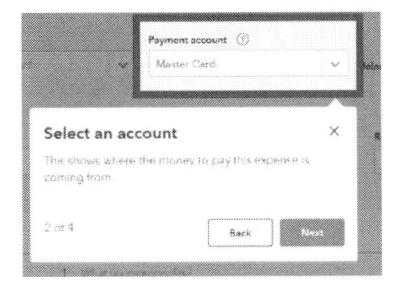

5. Enter the date of the expense in the **Payment date** field.

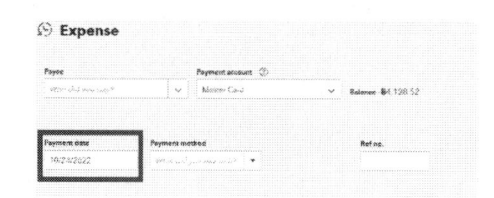

6. Select how you paid for the expense in the **Payment method** field.

7. Enter a Ref number or Permit number if you want to track something in detail. This is optional.

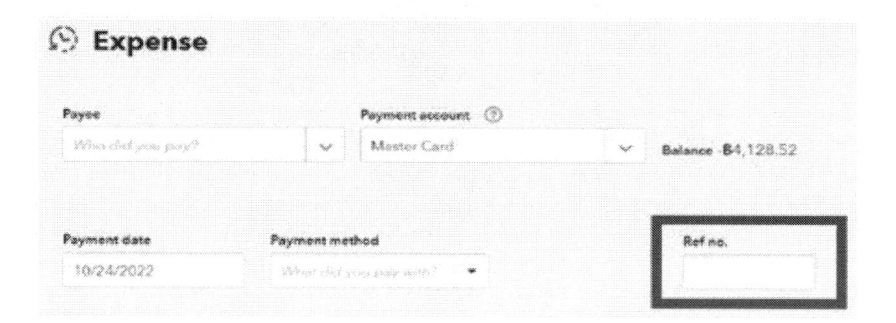

8. Enter the information about the expense in the section for **Category** details. In the **Category** dropdown menu, select the account you use to keep track of your expenses. It helps to place the item into the suitable tax category. Then you can write a description which tells what you paid for.

9. You can always choose to **Add lines** or **Clear all lines** if you must. Along that bar, you can see the total expenses.
10. Add a **Memo** or **Attachments** if you want to show them in printing or document the expense.
11. There are more options to choose from at the bottom of the expense window. You can **Print**, or click **More** if you want to **Copy**, **Void**, **Delete**, go to **Transaction journal** or **Audit History**.
12. When you're finished **click Save and close**, but you can also click the **dropdown** and select **Save and New**.

There are various types of expenses that cover many ranges of items and services you purchase and should be useful for your expenses' transactions in QuickBooks Online.

- Advertising/Promotional - The type of expenses spent on promotional materials like ads and business cards
- Bad Debts - Any loans or unpaid balances that can't be collected
- Bank Charges - Includes any bank fees on your banking transactions
- Commissions and fees - This is a type of expenses that covers clearing and settlement, custody, and securitization
- Computer Software and Hardware - The cost of purchasing software and hardware requirements of your products or services
- Dues and subscriptions - Professional dues, newspapers, and service subscriptions related to running your business

- Equipment rental - Renting machinery to develop a product or service
- Income tax expense - Fees for income tax like a State Income Tax or a Federal Income Tax
- Insurance (Disability) - Payment for income support benefits program for workers who are disabled and unable to work
- Insurance (General) - Insurance payment for business property damage, company vehicle, and so on
- Insurance (Liability) - Payment for liability insurance that protects a company's or business owner's finances if they are sued or if a third party makes a claim against them
- Interest expense - Interest on a mortgage, interest on a loan, or fees on a credit card
- Legal and professional fees - Expenses for paying professionals like Accountants, lawyers, or consultants to help you run your business
- Loss on discounted operations, net of tax - Including gain (loss) on disposal, provision (or reversals of earlier provisions) for loss on disposal, and prior period gain (loss) on disposal.
- Management compensation - Compensation paid for business officers
- Meals and entertainment - Expenses for food for client lunches, social events, and meals on the road
- Office expenses - Expenses for general or office-related expenses including supplies and furniture.
- Other selling expenses - Fees incurred for selling, usually by Sales department
- Payroll expenses - Payment for workers compensation and payroll taxes
- Rent or lease payments - Rent or lease of building expenses
- Repairs and Maintenance - Any vehicle, equipment, landscaping, and other periodic maintenance expenses.
- Shipping and delivery expense - The charge for transporting goods to distributors or consumers.
- Stationery and printing - Stationery and printing expenses for products or services of your business
- Supplies - Raw materials utilized to make a product or provide a service.
- Travel expenses (general and admin expenses) - Travel costs for food you eat while traveling, accommodation or trip ticket.

- Travel expenses (selling expenses) - Travel expenses for selling products
- Uncategorized Expense - A default account for unknown expenses
- Utilities - Payments for gas and electricity, water, telephone, and so on
- Wage expenses - Expenses for gross wages and salaries

HOW TO MANAGE EXPENSES

Tracking expenses and making timely payments are two of the most important tasks you can do with QuickBooks Online. What's more, you can organize your expenses easily. Alter the expenses you enter into QuickBooks by editing details or even deleting unwanted expenses.

Edit expenses

1. Go to the **Expenses** from the sidebar menu and click the **Expenses** tab.
2. Navigate to the expenses you want to edit and select **View/Edit** under the Action column.
3. You can edit the details in the highlighted fields.

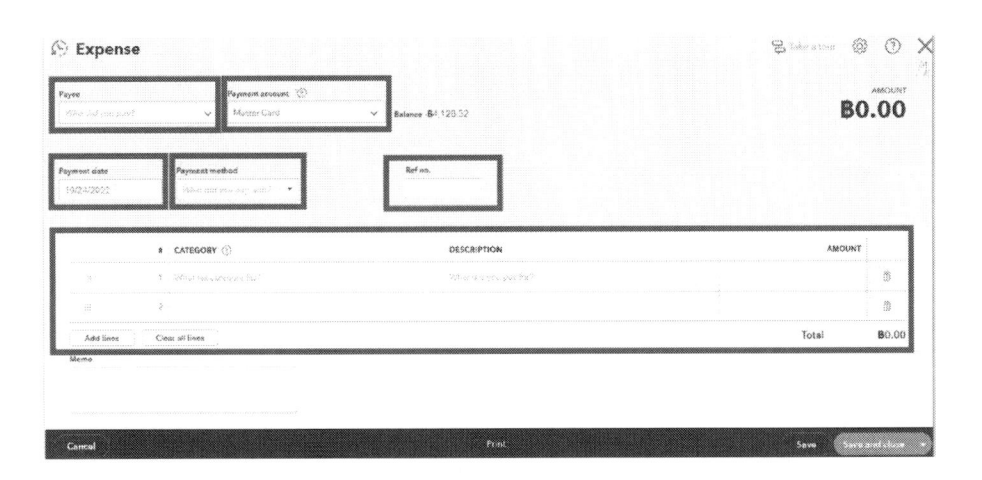

4. Select **Save and Close** when you're done editing.

Delete expenses

1. Go to the **Expenses** from the sidebar menu and click the **Expenses** tab.
2. Navigate to the expenses you want to delete and select the **dropdown** next to View/Edit under the Action column.
3. Select **Delete**.
4. Select **Yes**.

When an expense is deleted, it is removed from reports but is still visible in the Audit log.

HOW TO RECORD CHECK

Your QuickBooks checking account remains organized as long as you write and record checks for your expenses. You must enter a check in QuickBooks if you want to print a new check or make a purchase using a handwritten check.

Doing this as best practice makes sure that all of your business transactions are recorded and that your accounts are up to date

1. Select **+ New** from the side navigation bar.
2. Click the Check tab under the Vendors section.
3. Select the vendor in the **Payee** field.

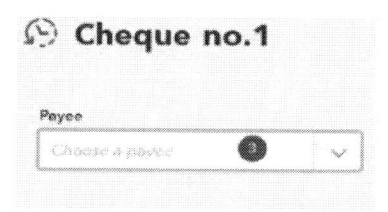

4. Click the **Bank account** dropdown then select the account you used to pay for the check.

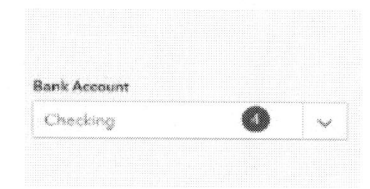

5. Enter the information for **Mailing** and **Date** fields.

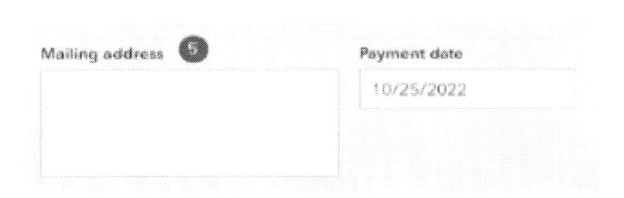

6. Write down the details about the check in the section for Category details. In the Category dropdown menu, select the account you use to keep track of your check. Then you can write a description which indicates what you paid for.

7. If you want to immediately open the queue for printing check, choose **Print** or **Preview**. Alternatively, if you want to print the check later, tick the **Print later** box.

8. Select **Save and close** once done. If you need to create another check, you can click **Save and new**.

Note: If you click **Save**, the check is added to your bank register; however, if you select **Print later**, the check is just sent to the print queue. If all you're doing is recording a handwritten check, you're done as soon as you save the check. Your check is available for printing from the print queue if you chose the **Print later** or **Print** or **Preview** option.

ADD BILLS AND BILL PAYMENTS

You may get an overview of unpaid invoices and spending using QuickBooks Online Essentials (and succeeding plans), track your bills, and pay them on time. Maintain control over your company's financial flow and keep track of all accounts payable. Build strong relationships with suppliers to avoid late payments.

Add a Bill Manually

1. Select **+ New**.
2. Select **Bill** under Suppliers.
3. Select a vendor from the **Vendor** dropdown menu.

Bill

Supplier: Art Wallace

4. Choose the terms of the bill from the **Terms** dropdown. Note that "Net" is the number of days until the payment is due in the Terms field.
5. Type the **Bill date**, **Due date**, and **Bill no.** exactly as they appear on the bill.

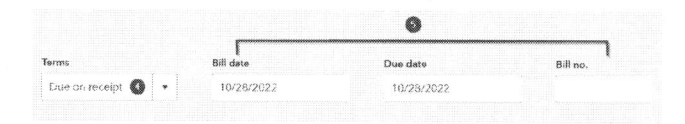

Terms: Due on receipt | Bill date: 10/28/2022 | Due date: 10/28/2022 | Bill no.

6. Fill out the **Category details** with the bill information. Select the cost account you use to keep track of spending transactions from the **Category** selection. Add a **Description** on the selected item.

#	CATEGORY	DESCRIPTION
1	Equipment rental	Automatic Linen Cutter
2		

7. Type in the **Amount**.

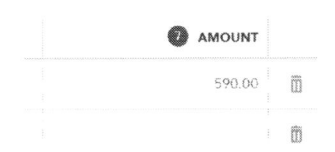

Note: If you want to bill customers for the expenses, select the **Billable** checkbox and type the customer's name in the **Customer** field

8. After finishing, choose **Save and close**.

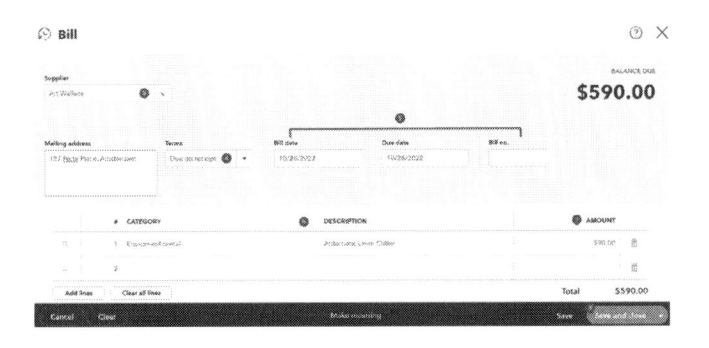

Importing Bills

The steps to importing files from your computer makes your billing management easy, especially if you have a bulk to upload, as shown in "Chapter Two - Importing spreadsheets and desktop data." You can import bills from your desktop through the **gear icon > Import data > Bills**.

Pay Bills Online

1. Select **+New** then **Pay bills**.
2. Select a bill. The checkbox for one or more bills can be selected.

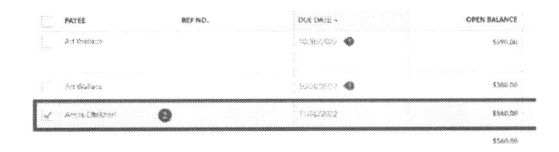

3. Then decide how you'll pay this bill. You can pay with a **debit** or **credit card** for a small cost or for free using your **bank** account. Keep in mind that the first time you do this, you'll need to connect with your bank.

4. After checking your payment, click **Save and close**.

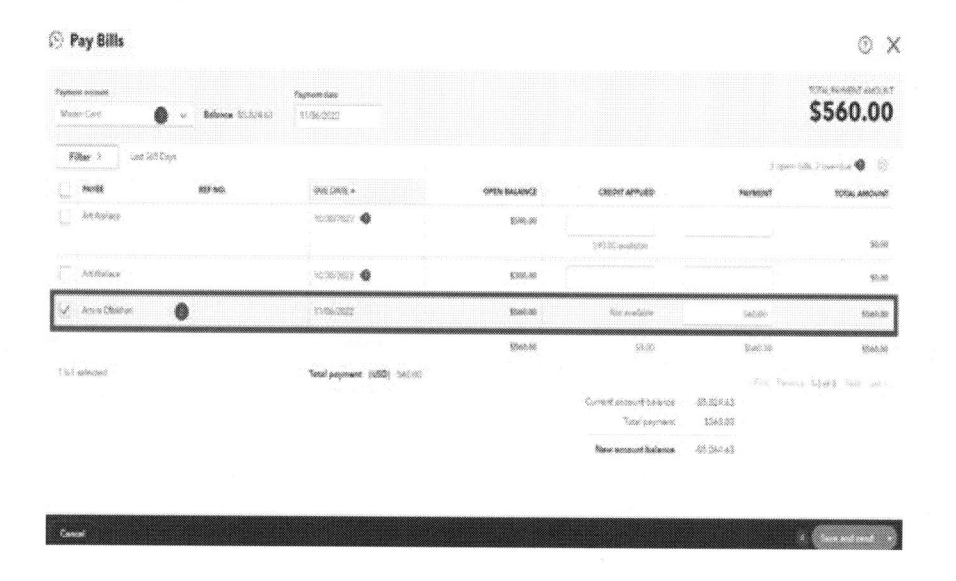

5. Click **Transactions** under the **Bookkeeping** menu. Locate the transaction that your bank has downloaded.

6. You'll notice that QuickBooks has a record of the bill you've already input for this transaction

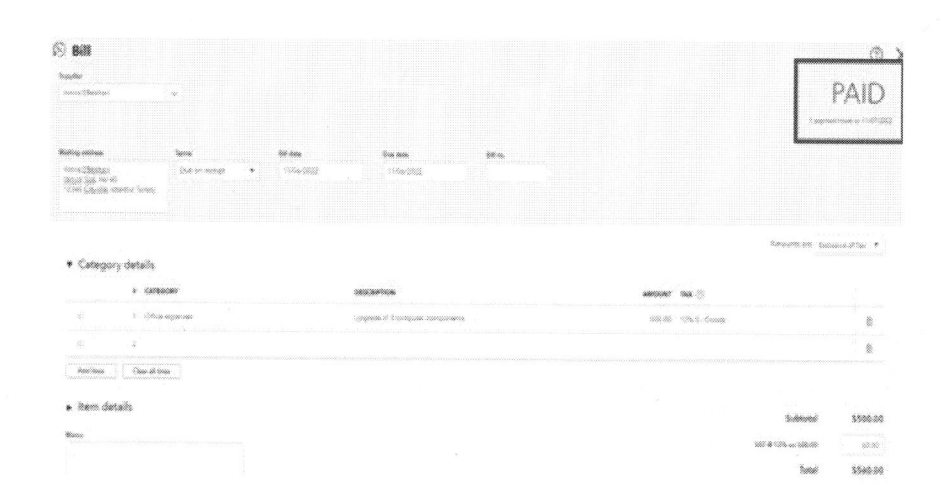

05

INVOICING

An invoice is a time-stamped record that itemizes and documents a buyer-seller transaction and plays an essential role in sales. Many small businesses turn to small business accounting software like QuickBooks Online (QBO) for its convenience of use and smart features in invoicing.

With online invoicing, you can create and send invoices right from a mobile app or cloud application. As a result, you won't ever have to be concerned about losing an invoice before it is recorded, and your sales data will always be current. Additionally, it does away with the necessity of keeping hard copies.

One more thing is that the system enables your sales team to create and deliver an invoice in just a few short minutes. You can get paid more quickly because instant delivery reduces the waiting period.

The invoice is tracked by QuickBooks from the minute it is issued to the client, allowing you to know precisely when the customer opens the invoice and even set up notifications to alert you when it has been fully paid. For a small business, investing in online invoicing can be very beneficial. Once configured in your accounting software, this function makes billing quick and affordable.

CREATE AND CUSTOMIZE AND INVOICE

Online invoicing in QuickBooks can save time, minimize mistakes, and maximize your budget if you produce a lot of sales. But that's not all, you can also build a personalized invoice that will show off the look of your brand and business by designing custom templates, adding a new logo, applying new colors and fonts, or updating your invoices with a signature, stamp, or QR code.

1. Select **+ New**.
2. Select **Invoice** under Customers.
3. Click **Add Customer**, then select a client from the **dropdown**. Enter the customer's email address.

4. Add the **Due Date**, **Terms**, and **Invoice Date**. Note that "Net" is the number of days until the payment is due in the Terms field.

5. Click **Add product or service** and choose an item from the selection.

6. To customize the design of your invoice, click **Customize**.

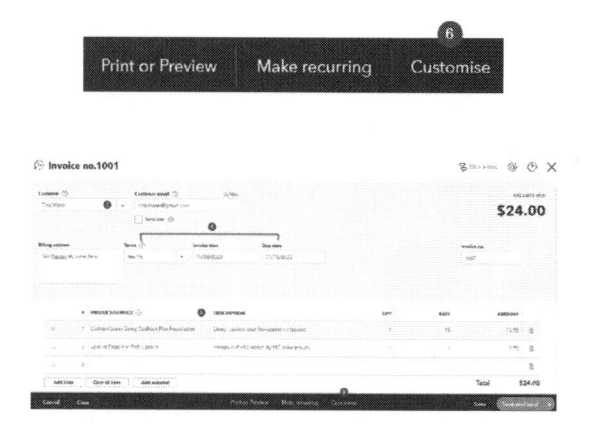

7. Select **New Style**. The customized window shows you different tabs.
8. The default tab is **Design** where you can select from the list of design options to customize.

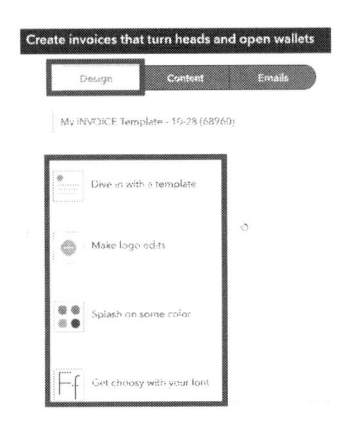

9. The next tab is **Content** that lets you edit information on your invoice.

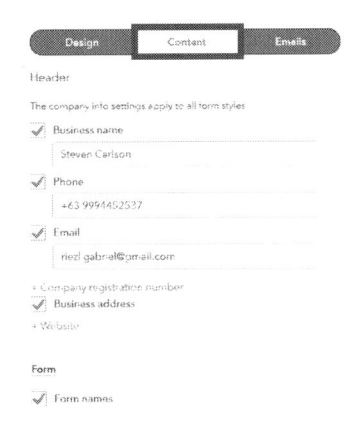

10. The **Emails** tab at the end is where you can change how your invoice appears in emails. Click **Done** to save your new invoice template.

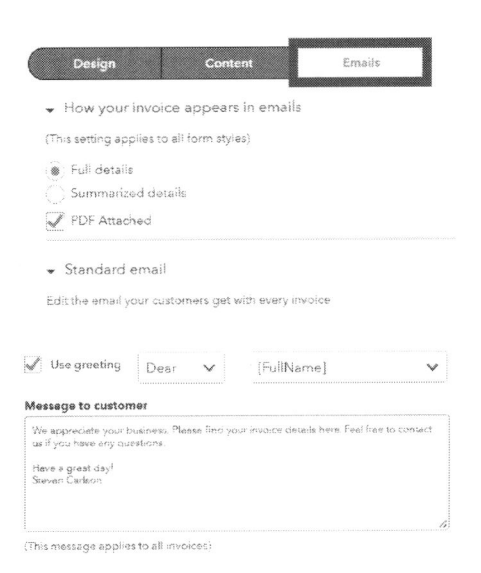

Your preferences are saved by QuickBooks, which then applies them to all current and upcoming invoices. When finished, you have several choices of saving or sending the invoice:

- Save and close
- Save and new
- Save and send
- Save and share link
- Save and share (WhatsApp)

HOW TO SEND INVOICE REMINDERS

When an invoice is past due, or about to be, you can send your clients reminders. Invoice due dates can be politely and easily prompted to clients. Automatic reminders can be set up in QuickBooks Online to be sent a few days before or after a payment is due. Rest assured that there will be an appropriate number of reminders to send out without your having to keep track of the dates yourself. Furthermore, the email can be tailored to your company's needs.

1. Click the **gear icon** then **click Account and settings**.
2. Choose the **Sales** tab.
3. Click **pencil icon** in the **Reminders** section.

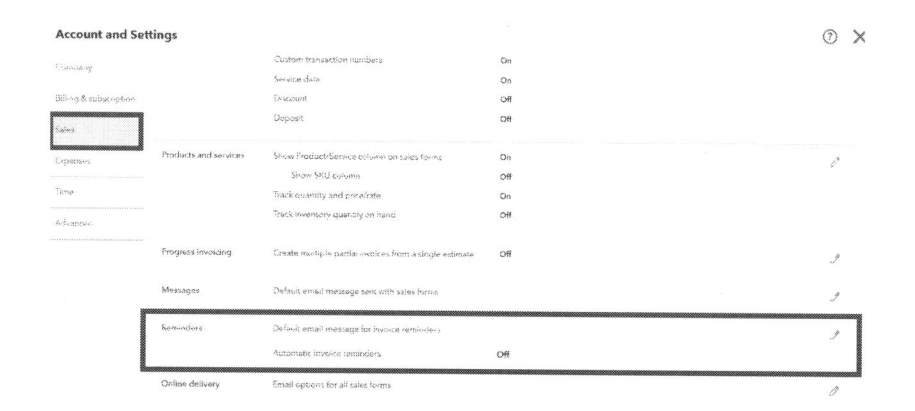

4. Enable **Automatic invoice reminders**.
5. Choose **Reminder 1** from the options.

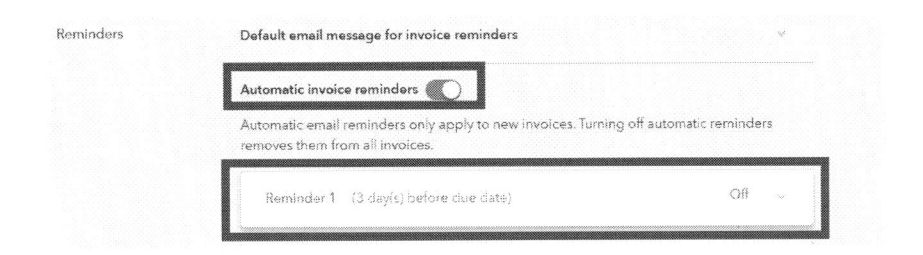

6. Toggle the switch to **ON**.

7. To inform QuickBooks when to issue the reminder, choose days, and either before or after from the selection boxes.

8. Edit the placeholders in your email

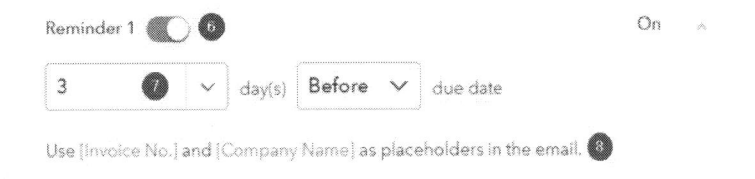

After enabling reminders, you can edit the message by customizing the email template as a reminder to meet your date settings.

9. Edit the subject line as necessary in the **Subject line** field.

10. To add a personalized welcome, tick the **Use email greeting box**. Choose a salutation from the **dropdown**.

11. Remove the message content from the **Email message** field and replace it with your own. You may also use the standard message.

12. If you want this message template as a default in every reminder, click **Use default reminder message**.

Reminder: Your payment to Steven Carlson is due ❾

☑ Use email greeting Dear [Full Name]

Email message

We're sending a reminder to let you know that invoice [Invoice No.] has not been paid. If you already paid this invoice or have any questions, let us know!

Have a great day!
Steven Carlson

Use default reminder message ⓬

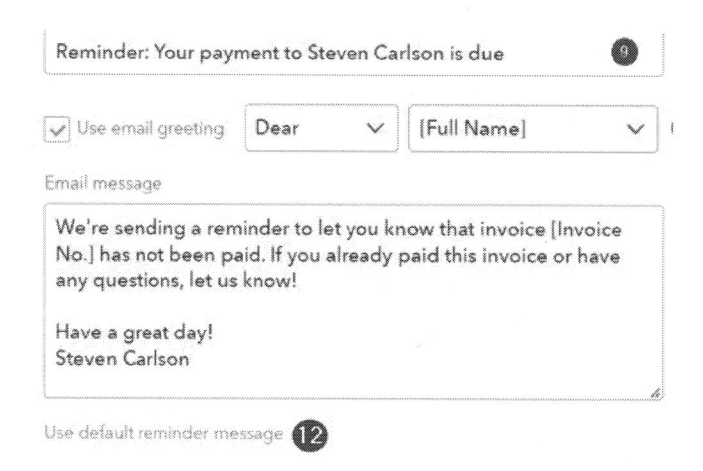

13. Click **Save**.

This serves as the model for all invoice reminders sent by QuickBooks. The due date on the form begins the countdown when you create an invoice. In invoicing, make sure the customer's email box contains an email address.

SALES AND REFUNDS

Sales are the quantity of goods and products that a business has sold, and as we all know, sales are the primary source of income for a business. Without sales, it won't be long before the money runs out to keep manufacturing, accounting, purchasing, and management operating. For an expanding business, keeping track of sales can be a real headache, but luckily, QuickBooks Online has you covered.

QuickBooks Online is a powerful tool to streamline your business and manage your sales and payments. It offers features that make it easy to view, create, and edit sales transactions in just a few clicks.

Get more out of QBO and let its sales functionality make it work for you by creating invoices, payments, sales receipts, estimates, and credit memos. Copy, delete, void, or print transactions with the ability to customize. Plus, process customers' and suppliers' refunds in no time.

You can see all of your transactions and invoice statuses in one place, including any outstanding or recently paid bills. Whether a transaction is Open, Closed, or Overdue may now be seen with a simple glance.

RECEIVE AND RECORD INVOICE PAYMENTS

More than ever, it's critical to track every payment entering your business and make sure it's put into proper accounts. QuickBooks Online provides a simple method for recording a customer payment so that the invoice is recognized as paid after processing. Regular payment recording keeps the invoice from being open and showing up as unpaid on your reports.

Record a Payment

1. Click **+ New** and click **Receive payment** under Customers.
2. Select the customer's name from the **Customer** dropdown.

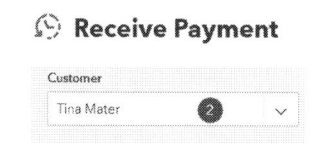

3. Select the payment option from the **Payment method** dropdown.

4. Select the account you want to deposit the money into from the **Deposit to** dropdown.

5. Tick the box next to the invoice you want to record the payment in the **Outstanding Transactions** section.

6. Note that if you want to record a "partial payment" for an invoice, you can edit the default amount in the **Amount received** field and enter the amount your customer paid.

7. After completing, choose **Save and close**.

Edit or Void an Invoice Payment

1. Go to the Sales menu and click the All Sales tab.
2. Select a transaction you want to manage and click View/Edit link. Click Save and close from the Save options at the bottom right.
3. If you want to void the transaction, click the dropdown then select Void.

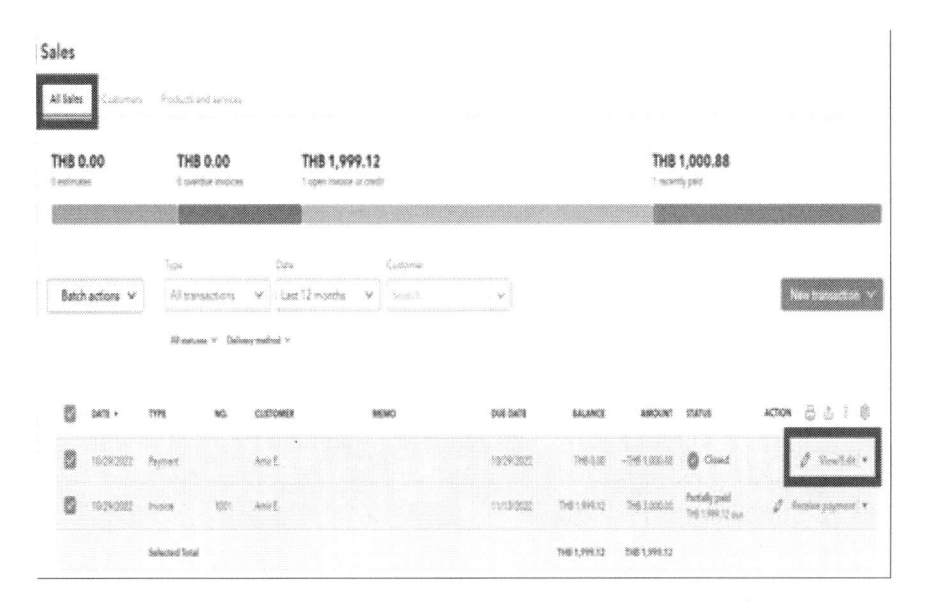

WHAT IS UNDEPOSITED FUNDS ACCOUNT AND HOW IS IT USED?

You can combine multiple checks and cash into one deposit in your check register by using the Undeposited Funds account. Without Undeposited Funds, each received payment appears in the check register as individual deposits, making it inconvenient to connect to the bank statement where checks are consolidated into a single deposit amount.

Let's imagine that you deposit five $1,000 checks from several clients into your actual checking account. Five checks totaling $5,000 are recorded by your bank as a single deposit. Therefore, to match your $5,000 bank deposit, you must merge your five different $1000 records in QuickBooks.

If you're downloading transactions directly from your bank, you don't need to do this.

How does it work?

Use Undeposited Funds to match your deposit slip and combine your online banking payments. Doing this ensures that your bank records always match, making reconciliations much simpler. Merge several payments into a single deposit with Undeposited Funds feature in QuickBooks.

1. Click **+ New** and select **Receive Payment** under Customers.
2. Select a **Customer** from the dropdown.

3. Select a **Payment method**.
4. Select **Undeposited Funds** in Deposit to field.

5. Click on **Save and New** and add each payment.

RECORD A BANK DEPOSIT

After you receive checks and put them into your Undeposited Funds account, you may now collect them and put them together to make a single deposit. It is considered a best practice to record a deposit into QuickBooks Online in order to keep track of any transactions made through your bank account. Recording your deposits maintains your bank transactions current and correct.

1. Click **+ New** and select **Bank deposit** under Other.
2. Select an **Account** from the dropdown.

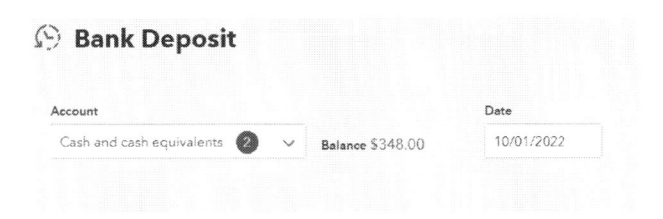

3. Tick the box of each payment you want to select the payments included in this deposit.

4. Click on **Save and Close**.

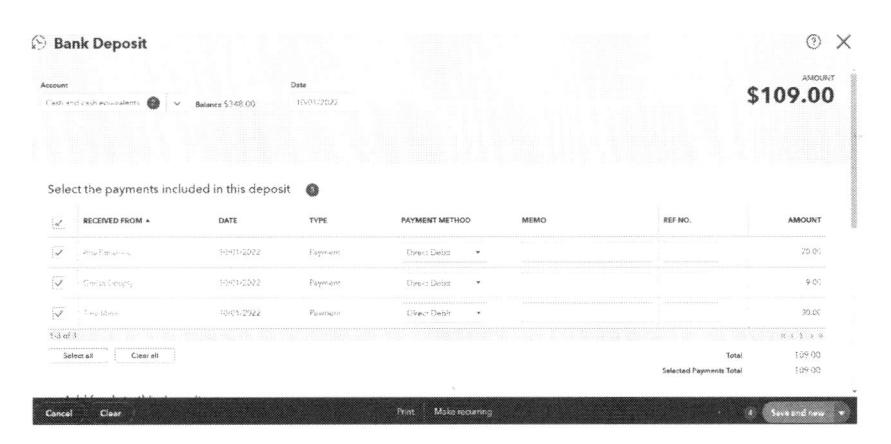

RECORD A REFUND

How to Record a Customer Refund

In case you need to return a payment to a customer, QuickBooks lets you record a refund transaction.

1. Click **+ New** and select **Credit note** under Customers.
2. Select the customer you want to give a refund to in the **Customer** field **dropdown**.

3. Enter the **Service Date** and the **Product/Service**.

4. Select **Save and close**.

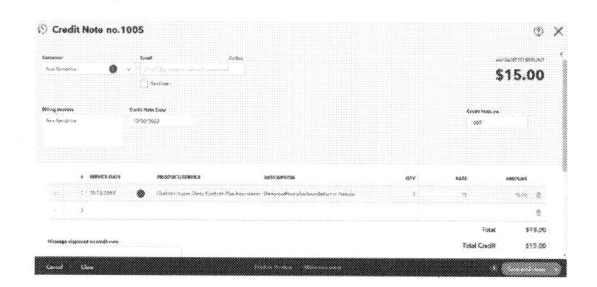

Note: There is no need for vendor credit for overpaid type of refunds.

5. Click **+ New** and select **Expense** under Suppliers.

6. Select the same customer in the **Payee** field.

7. Select the bank where the money is being refunded from in the **Payment account** field.

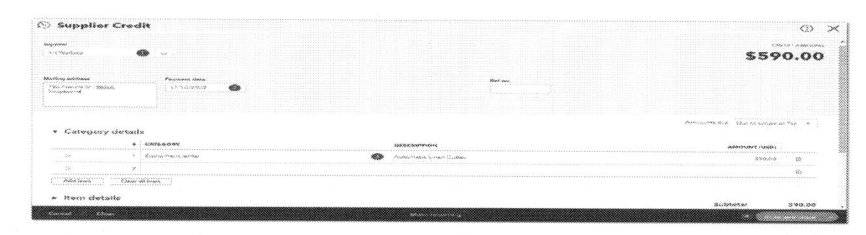

8. Select the **Debtors** account in the **Category** field.

9. Enter the refund amount in the **Amount** field.

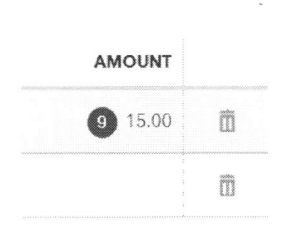

10. Select **Save**.

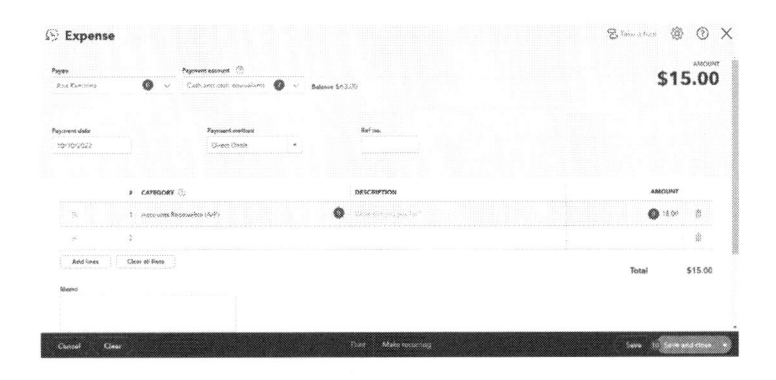

11. Next, go to **+New** and select **Receive payment** under Customers.

12. Add the same **Customer** and select the **Payment method** and **Deposit to**.

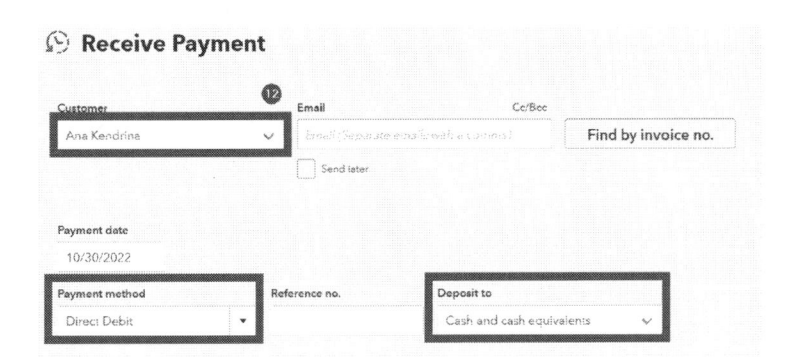

13. The outstanding transaction as well as the credit are both marked checked by default. As this is a refund process, the end result should have a 0 balance in order to cancel the transaction.

14. Select **Save and close**.

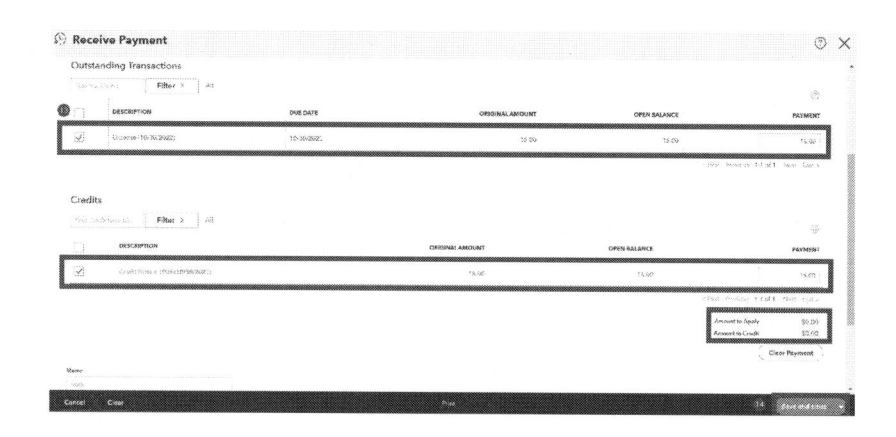

HOW TO RECORD A SUPPLIER REFUND

1. Click **+ New** and select **Supplier credit** under Suppliers.
2. Select the supplier paying for the refund in the **Supplier** field.
3. Enter the **Payment date**.

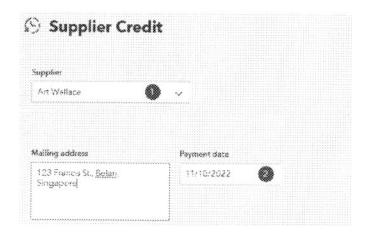

4. Enter the **Category** and **Amount**.

5. Select Save and close.

6. There is no need for supplier credit to be shown for overpaid type of refunds. Click **+ New**.
7. Select **Bank deposit** under Other.
8. Click the **Add funds to this deposit** and enter the following information in this section.
9. Select the supplier paying for the refund in the **Received From** field.
10. Select the **Accounts Payable** or create a "Creditors" account in the Account field

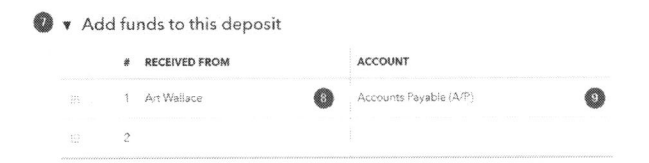

11. Add a **Payment Method**.
12. Enter the refund amount in the **Amount** field.

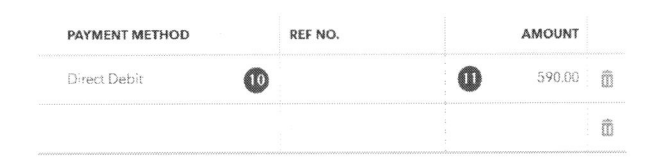

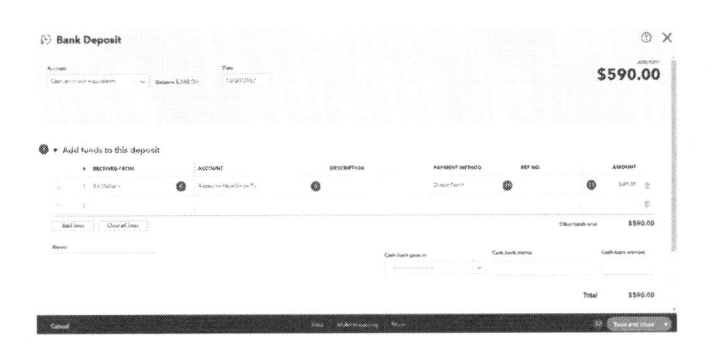

13. Select **Save and close**.

14. Go to **+ New** and select **Check** under Suppliers.
15. Add a **Payee**. This should be the supplier who paid for your refund.

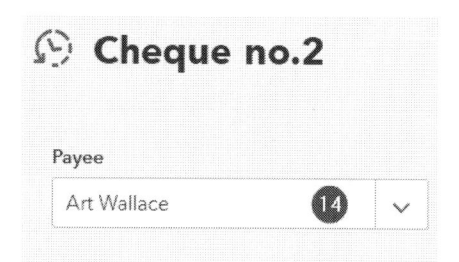

16. On the **Add Bill Payment** on the right-side panel, add the transactions you want to include. In this case, they should be the **Deposit refund** and the **Supplier credit**.

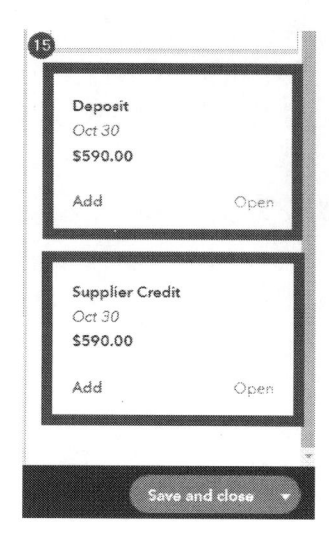

17. The end result should have a 0 balance to cancel the transaction.

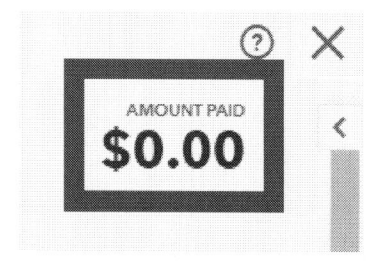

18. Select **Save and close.**

How to Manage Credit Card Refunds

1. Click **+ New** and select **Credit card credit** under Suppliers.
2. Select a vendor in the **Payee** field.
3. Select the credit card from where the money is being refunded from in the **Bank/Credit account** dropdown.
4. Enter the **Payment date**.

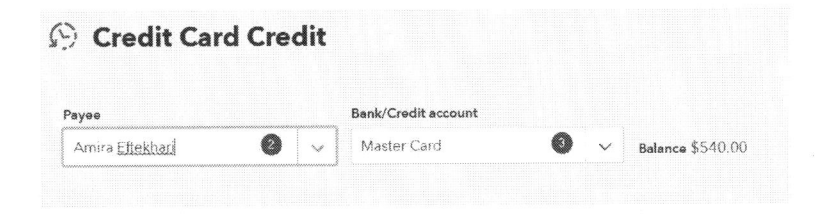

5. Enter the **Category** and refund Amount.

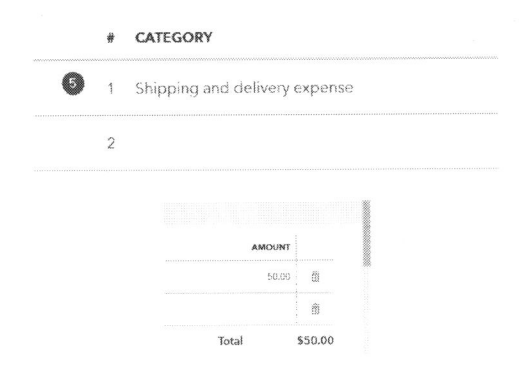

6. Select **Save and close**.

07

PAYROLL

Payroll refers to a company's financial records pertaining to its employees or the distribution of wages to those employees. If you have employees and need to pay them, administer their benefits, calculate, and withhold taxes automatically, or set up a regular pay schedule, QuickBooks Online (QBO) can help.

QuickBooks Online Payroll is an add-on software to QBO that helps with payroll processing and other accounting tasks. Payroll processing includes calculating employees' salaries, automating pay methods, covering HR support and benefits, and withholding the appropriate amount for federal and state payroll taxes. This feature syncs with accounting and can be added to your existing QuickBooks plan so you can manage everything in one place.

HOW TO SET UP PAYROLL AND ADD EMPLOYEES

When you use QuickBooks Payroll, you won't have to put in as much effort to keep track of when your paycheck is due. It alerts you when your next paycheck is due. In addition, it is useful for estimating wages and other costs associated with a project.

QuickBooks makes it simple to comply with payroll and tax reporting requirements by adding, organizing, and managing employee data. Thus, fewer people are needed to carry out such administrative tasks. If you have an add on Payroll feature to your current QuickBooks Online plan, all you have to do is follow the on-screen prompts to complete some tasks needed for the set up.

1. Click the **Payroll** tab on the left navigation bar.

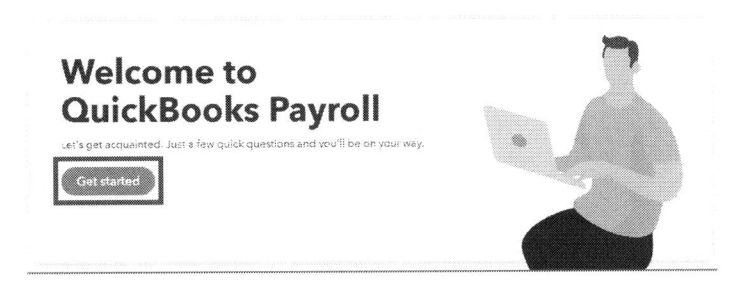

2. Follow the prompt on the screen and provide the required information to process payroll set up.

3. To add employees, you have the option to add them manually by clicking **Add Employee** or import a file for adding bulk employee lists with **Upload your report**.

4. If you choose to add an employee manually, a window appears on the screen requiring the employee's information. Fill out the required fields.

5. Toggle **Employee self-setup** if you want QuickBooks to send your new employee an invite to QuickBooks Workforce and let them enter their personal details, tax, and banking information.

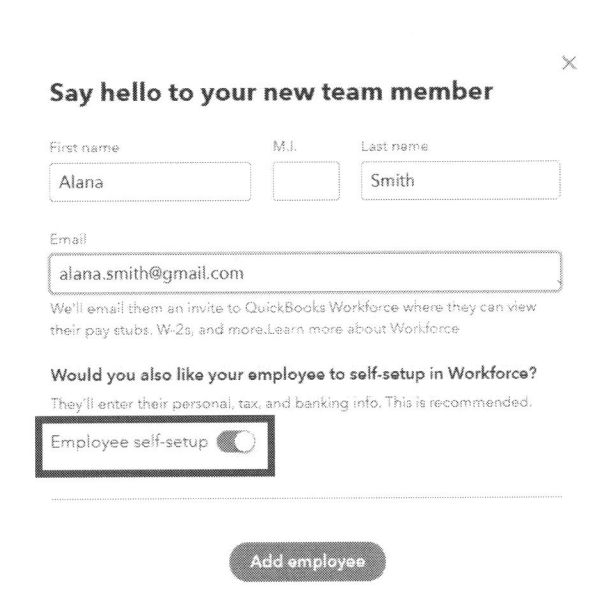

6. Click **Add employee**.

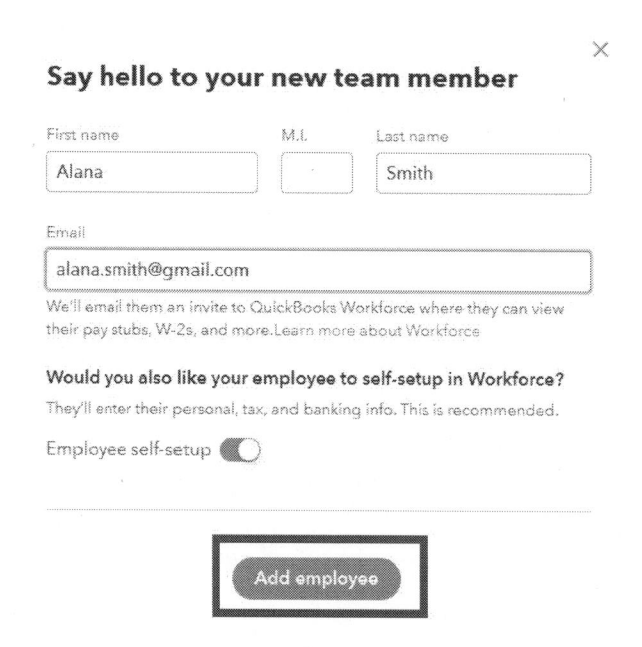

7. The employee you just added has a page that needs additional information to be completed such as personal info, pay type, employment details and pay method. Tip: You can exit this page for now to set up other tasks then return here later.

8. Click **Done**.

Finish configuring QuickBooks Payroll through tasks and adding employees to run payroll.

HOW TO PAY EMPLOYEES USING DIRECT DEPOSIT

Direct deposit pay method is available for free with QuickBooks Online Payroll. Employers will find it simple to conduct unlimited payroll runs for the employees who are already registered with the software.

You can pay your employees additional hourly rates or wages, bonuses, commissions, overtime, and fringe benefits in addition to their regular salary or hourly rate of pay.

Set up direct deposit

1. Use Instant Bank Verification to link your bank account, then immediately use direct deposit for your team.

    A. If you are new to payroll, click **Payroll,** then click **Start**.

    B. Click **Get Started.**

    C. Go to bank account and click **Review.**

4. Select your bank from the list.

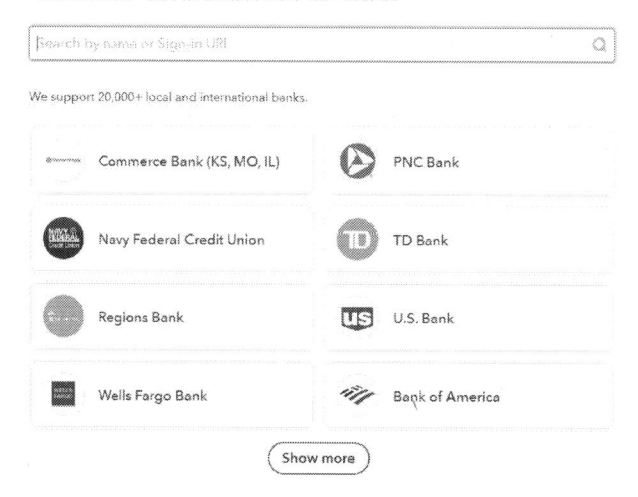

E. Sign in your account. Follow the prompts on the screen.

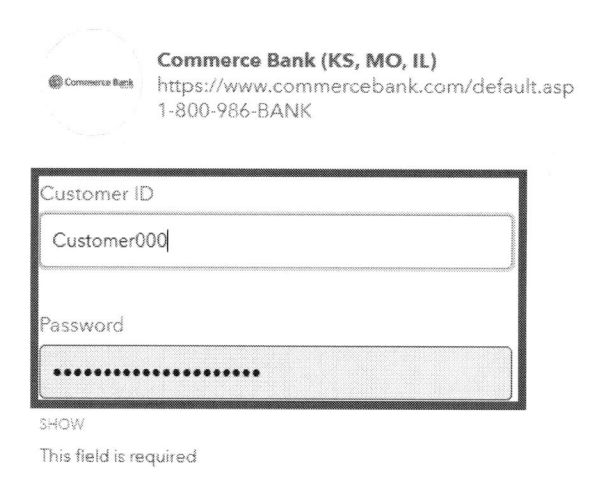

You will receive a success notification once you have attained the connection of the required bank account.

2. If your bank account can't be immediately accessed, QuickBooks sends a test debit of less than $1.00. To authorize your account for payroll transactions, enter that sum. You might not see that debit for up to two days.

Apply direct deposit to your payroll

1. Click **Employees** tab, under **Payroll** menu.

2. Select the name of the employee.

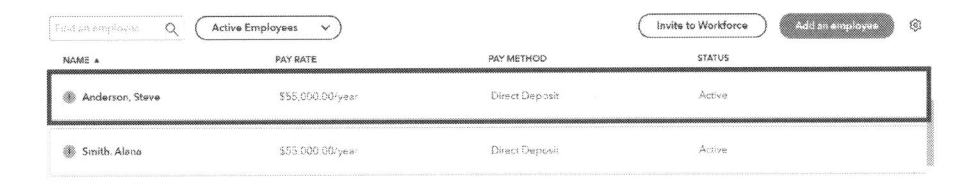

3. Under **Pay method**, click the **Edit** icon.

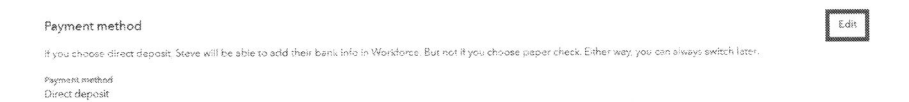

4. Select **Direct deposit** as the pay method then **Save**.

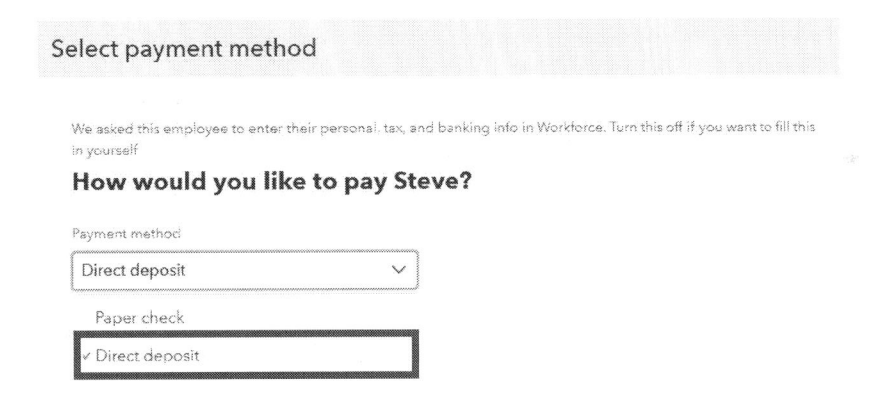

5. Select a type of **Direct deposit.**

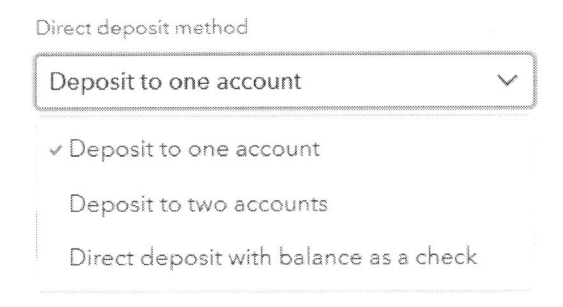

6. Select the **Bank account type**, **Routing number**, **Account number**, **Confirm account number**. Click **Save**.

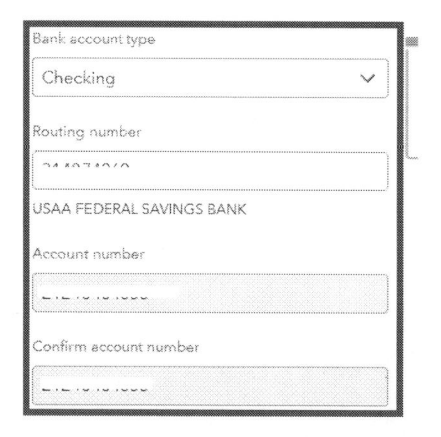

CREATING A TIMESHEET FOR EMPLOYEES

You can easily create a timesheet for employees, in addition to being able to link their pay to their information and pay method. This software also makes it much easier to make reports on how much a job cost. The funds will be sent directly to the employee's bank account.

Create a weekly timesheet

1. Click **+New**, then click **Weekly Timesheet** under **Employees**.
2. Select the **Name** of the employee.
3. Select the date of the week you want to create a timesheet for.
4. Select a **Customer**.
5. Enter the **Job and Service Item**.
6. Enter the salary item details.
7. Tick the **Billable** box if the hours worked can be billed.
8. Tick the **Taxable** box if applicable.

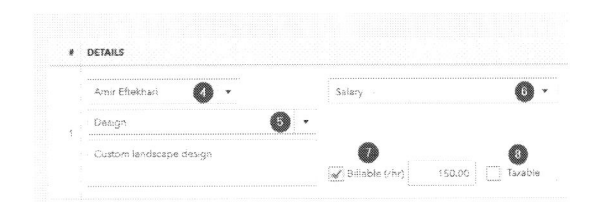

9. Choose the day the hours were worked and write down the hours worked for this job (if it was used) and/or for the payroll item.

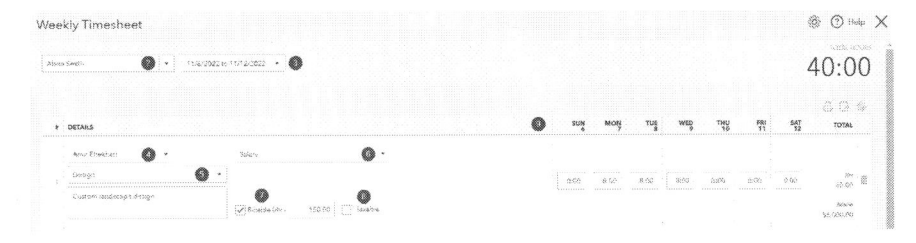

10. Work this method till the end of the week by repeating this each time. Neither the number of hours worked, nor the entire timesheet can currently be copied in QuickBooks. Each employee's hours must be completed one at a time.

11. You can get the timesheet information for each employee from the most recent time they put in by clicking the **Copy Last Sheet** button in the top left corner. There is a weekly limit of one timesheet per person.

12. Click the dropdown to **Save & Close**.

Create a single activity timesheet

1. From the Date calendar, select the working date.

2. Select the employee from the dropdown list for **Name**.

3. Select a pay item.

4. Select a customer job from the **Customer/Project** dropdown and service item from the **Service Item** dropdown to determine whether the hours spent are billable.

5. Click **Billable**. Don't select the checkbox if the item isn't billable.

6. Tick the **Taxable** box if applicable.

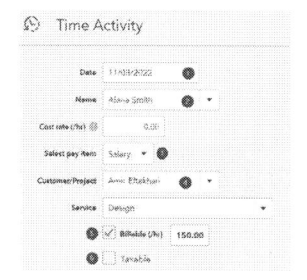

7. Enter a time.

8. Click **Save & Close**.

If you have independent contractors, remember that you'll need to fill out a 1099-NEC form for each of them at the end of the year and send it to both the contractors and the IRS. Independent contractors are self-employed people or businesses who are hired by another business to do work or provide services as a non-employee. In Chapter Nine: Taxes of this guide, you can learn more about how to make and file a 1099 form.

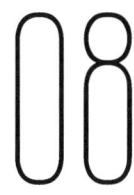

TRACKING & MANAGEMENT

Inventory tracking can be time-consuming for many small and medium-sized businesses. QuickBooks online inventory management software helps you effectively manage your inventory, so you always know what stock you have and what you need before you even need it.

Here are some advantages of the inventory tracking and management feature of QuickBooks Online:

1. QuickBooks stock inventory management software immediately reflects changes to your stock as items are received and shipped. That way, it's simple to identify what's moving and what needs replenishing.
2. It monitors the real stock price as it happens. Your financial statement will reflect the current value of your stock.
3. Keep track of what you have. You can sort your products into categories and set prices for them, and use "first-in, first-out" to automatically figure out how much each item sold costs (FIFO).
4. Find out how well each item sells and whether or not it's worth keeping in stock. Get fast access to top-selling items, sales figures, and tax tally with a few clicks of the mouse by running sales reports.

Stock features are available for QuickBooks Online Plus. If you don't have Plus, upgrade your QuickBooks plan to start tracking your stock.

HOW TO START TRACKING YOUR STOCK

Real-time monitoring of stock levels is possible with QuickBooks Online's streamlined approach to inventory management. Maintain separate inventories for items that are and are not subject to taxation. Maintain an up-to-date record of all orders and what has been ordered from each vendor.

In order to add your stock, you'll need to activate the stock tracking options.

1. Click the **gear icon** and select **Account and settings**.
2. Click **Sales**.
3. In the **Products and services** section, click the **pencil icon**.

4. Enable **Show Product/Service Column** on sales forms.
5. Turn on **Track quantity and price/rate** and **Track stock quantity on hand**.
6. Click **Save**.
7. Click **Done**.

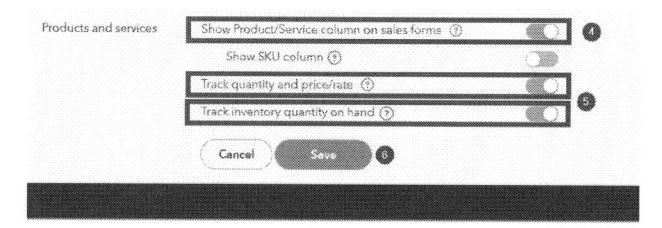

8. Add items to your stock that you want to track. You can go back to Chapter Two and see how to add new products and services to guide you.

Note: Keep in mind that QuickBooks only tracks stock items. Services, non-stock products, and bundles will not be tracked in terms of quantity.

After entering all of your in-stock items, you may monitor their sales. If you want to keep track of what you've sold and how much you've made, you may either create invoices or use sales receipts.

After an invoice or sales receipt is created, QuickBooks deducts the corresponding amount from available stock. As you prepare an invoice, a sales receipt, or any other form of transaction, you can view the stock and track anything that's still on backorder.

HOW TO REORDER INVENTORY FROM VENDORS WHEN LOW ON STOCK

QuickBooks will also alert you when anything is running low if you specify reorder points. You can avoid being behind on orders and reorder any items that are short in supply or unavailable.

Track the items as they arrive in order to keep your inventory updated.

1. Check for alerts on low stock or out-of-stock items. Select **Products and services** tab from **Get paid & pay or Sales menu**.

2. You can instantly identify if you have low stock or out-of-stock items at the top. To view those items, select **Low stock or Out of stock**. If something has reached or fallen below its "reorder point," or the point at which you should reorder new products, QuickBooks will know it is running low.

3. When you add new products, you can enter reorder points. You can edit those products to add them if your existing product has no reorder points.

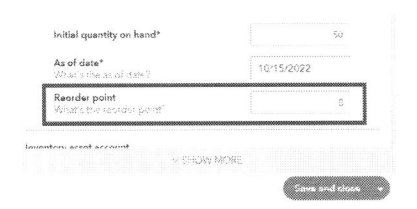

Next, prepare and send a purchase order. You can inform suppliers of the goods you require by sending them a purchase order. Make a purchase following these steps:

1. Click to **Sales** or **Get paid & pay**, then select **Products and services**.
2. Click **Out of Stock** or **Low Stock**. Do not use the top filters if you need to reorder both low stock and out of stock items from the same supplier.

3. Choose the products as required.
4. Click **Batch actions** and then click **Reorder**. This generates a single purchase order.

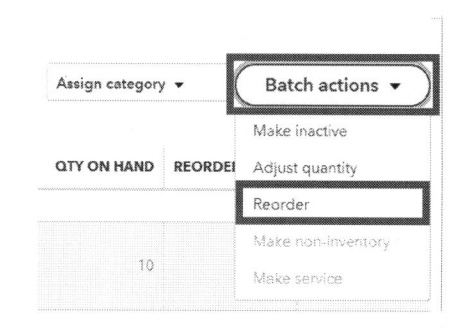

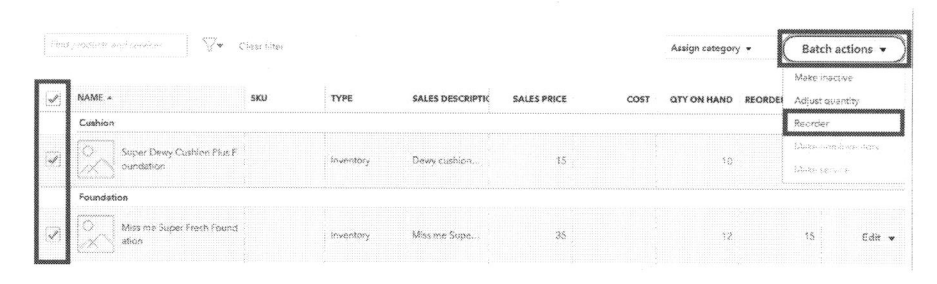

5. This process redirects you to Purchase Order. Finish filling out the purchase order completely or add additional items you need to have the seller replenish.
6. Click on **Save and send**.

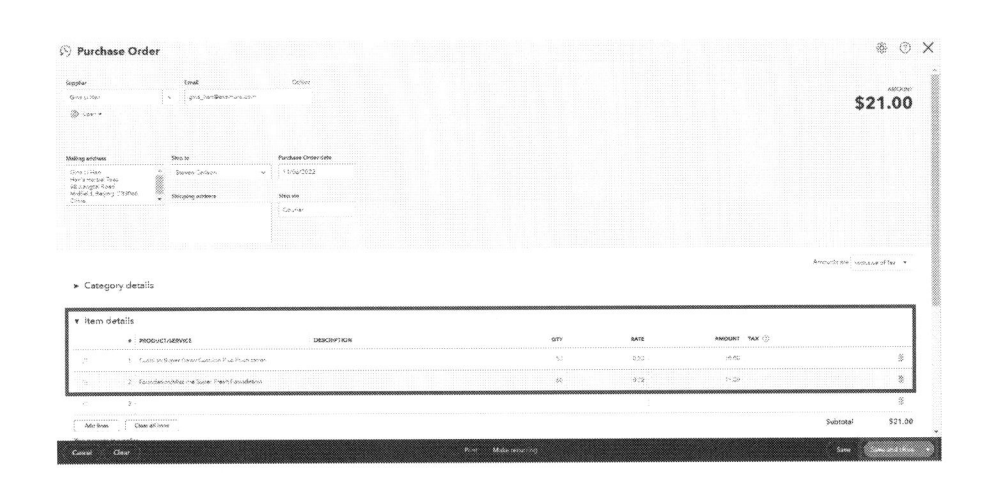

Check the items that are still on order to discover how many are there and how many have already been delivered. Click **Reports** and run **Open Purchase Order Detail report**.

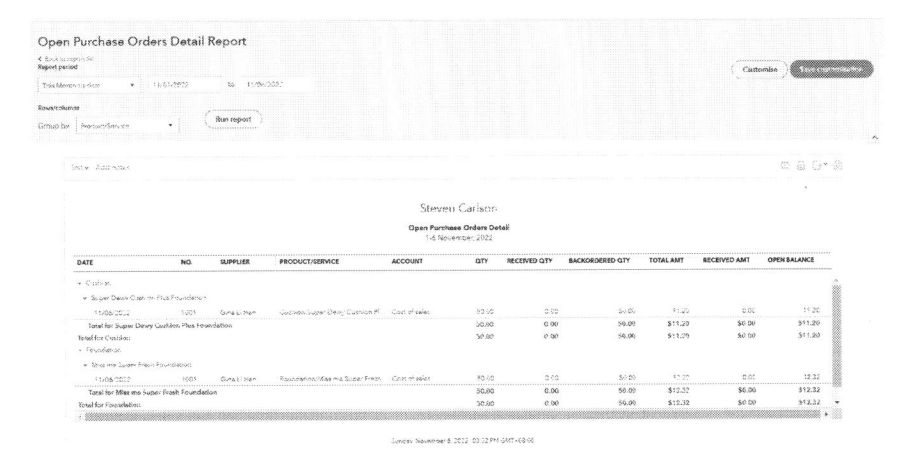

HOW TO CREATE PROJECTS AND START TRACKING THEM

Checking on a project's profitability is a breeze using QuickBooks Online's built-in "projects" feature. Income, expenditures, and labor costs for a project may all be entered in one place, and reports can be generated just for that project. You can even incorporate past purchases into active projects if necessary. The QuickBooks Online Plus and Advanced plans are the only ones that include the Projects feature.

TRACKING & MANAGEMENT

Create a new project

1. Navigate to **Business overview** and select **Projects**.
2. Click **New project**.

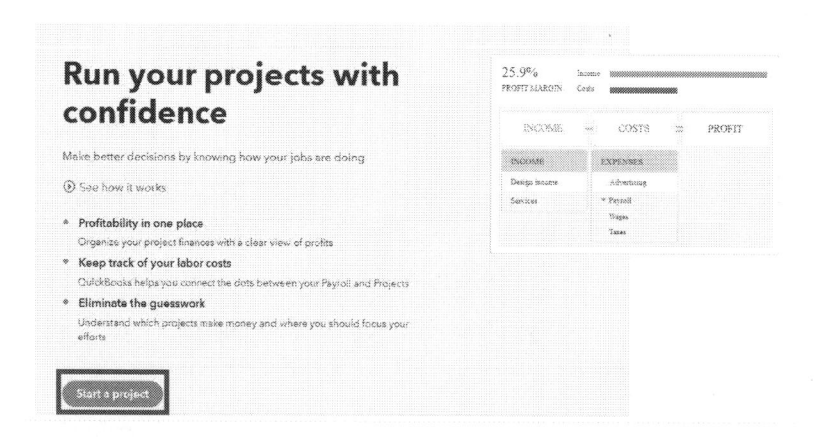

3. Type the project's title into the **Project name** text box.
4. From the **Customer** dropdown, select the client for this project.
5. Enter the **Start date** and **End date**.
6. Enter the **Project Status**.

7. You can write any relevant project notes in the **Notes** section.
8. Click **Save**.

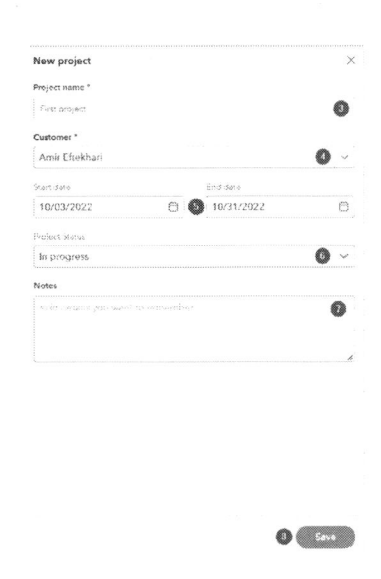

Add new transactions to a project

Add invoices, timesheets, or expenses to your QuickBooks projects. Projects' classification or impact on your accounts are unaffected by the addition of transactions. Projects simply allow you to keep track of its revenues and expense.

1. Click **Business overview** then **Projects**.
2. Click a **project**.

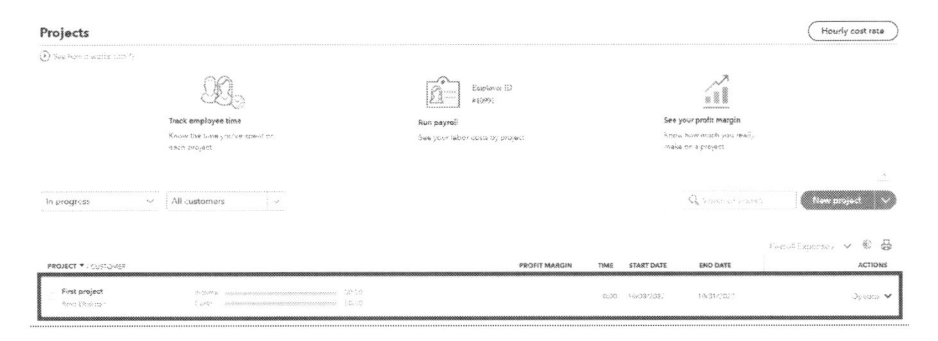

3. To add a new transaction, click **New project**.

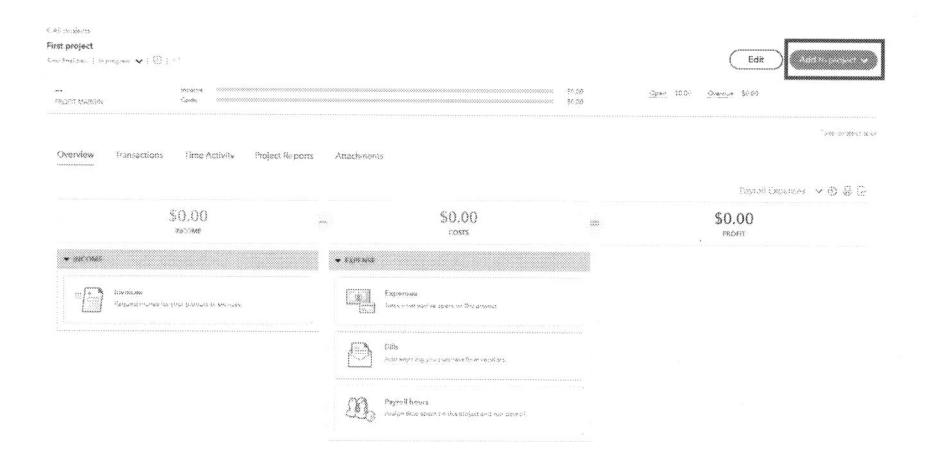

QUICKBOOKS ONLINE
FOR BEGINNERS, UPDATED EDITION

4. Select **Bill, Receive Payment, Expense, Estimate**, or **Invoice**.

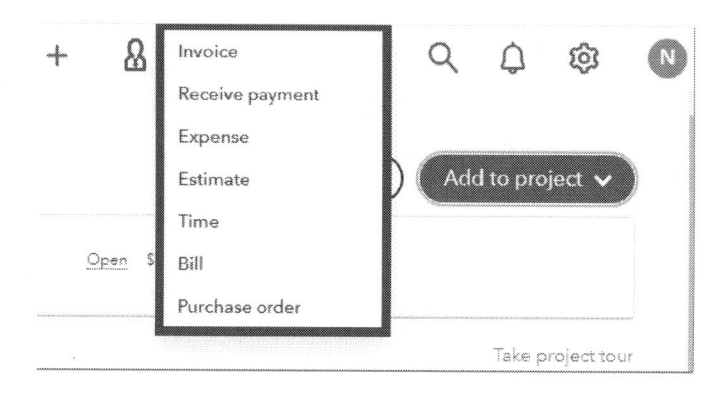

5. Fill out necessary details. **Save and close**.

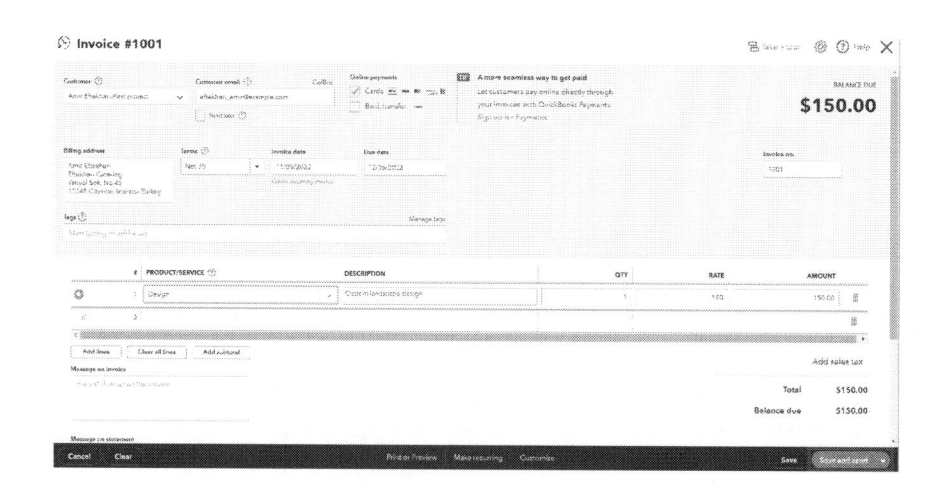

TRACKING & MANAGEMENT

Add existing expenses to a project

1. Click **Bookkeeping**, then click **Transactions**.
2. Click **Expenses**.
3. Select **Payee**.
4. Select **Payment account**.
5. Select **Payment method**.

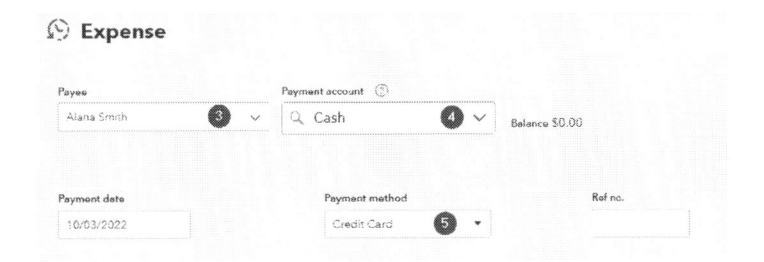

6. Click the **Category details** dropdown and enter the **Category**, **Amount**, and **Customer/Project**.

7. Tick the **Billable** box if the expense is billable to the customer.

8. If the expense is a product or service, click the **Item details** and enter the necessary information.
9. Choose **Save** and **close**.

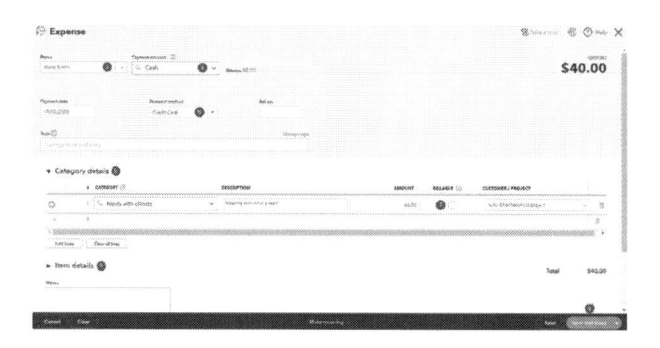

Add existing timesheets to a project

Depending on your account type, you can locate and add timesheets to a project from the Time menu or in the Weekly Timesheet even if they are not billable. This is so that you can monitor your profitability.

1. Click **+ New**.
2. Click **Weekly Timesheet**.
3. Choose the employee whose timesheets you want to add to the project from the **Employee** dropdown.
4. Choose the right week for the timesheets you're adding to the project from the date range dropdown.

5. Find the timesheets and click the **Customer or Project** dropdown. Select the project.

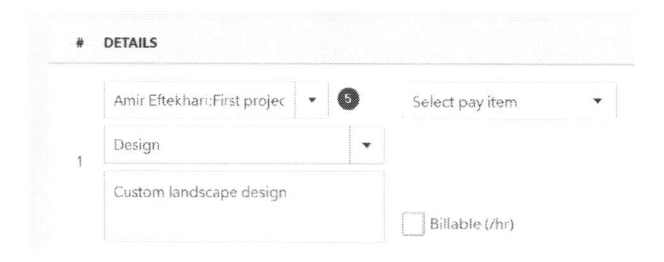

6. Click **Save**.

Add existing invoices to a project

A. Add unpaid invoices

1. Click **Get paid and pay** menu and click Invoices.
2. Select the unpaid invoice you want to add, then click the **pencil icon**.

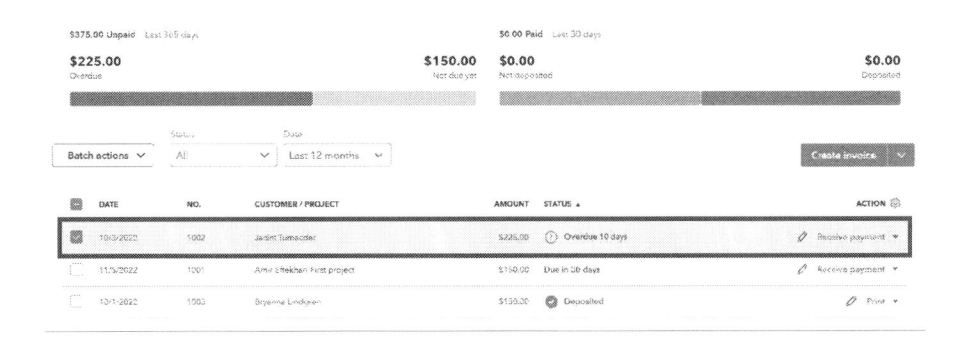

3. Select project from the **Customer** dropdown then **Save**.

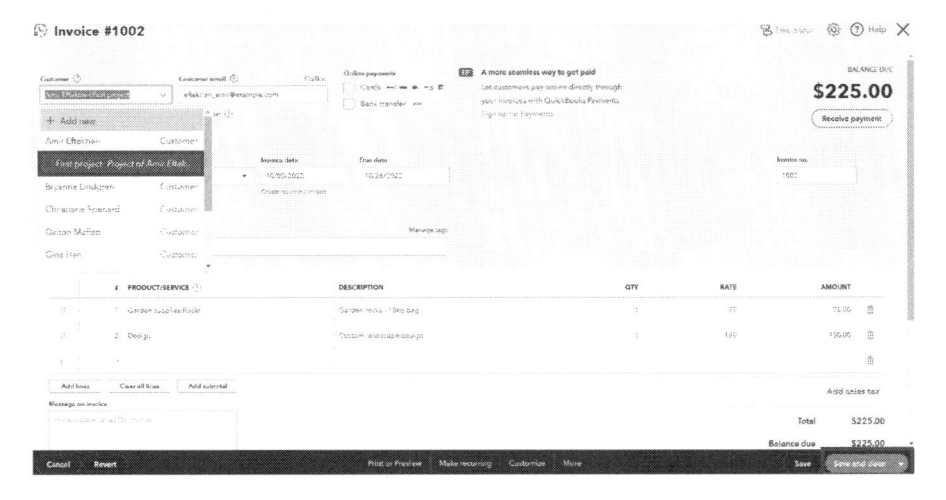

B. Add paid invoices

After a paid invoice is added to a project, it no longer links to the associated payment and is marked as unpaid. To avoid mistakenly charging the customer twice, you'll need to reconnect the payment to the invoice after making changes to the invoice.

1. Click **Get paid and pay** menu and click Invoices.
2. Select the paid invoice you want to add then click the **pencil icon**.

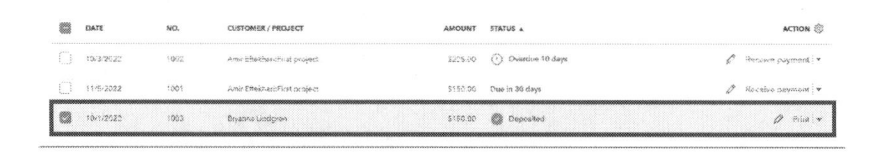

3. Select project from the **Customer** dropdown then **Save**.

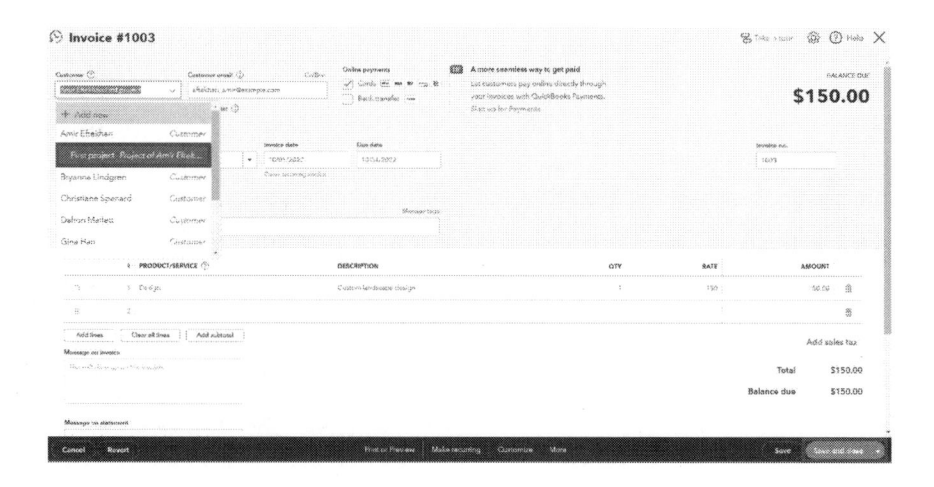

Reconnect the payment now that you've added the invoice to the project in order to record it as paid again and link it to the correct invoice.

1. Click the **gear icon** and select **Chart of accounts** under **Your Company**.
2. Select the account where the money was deposited. Click **View register**.

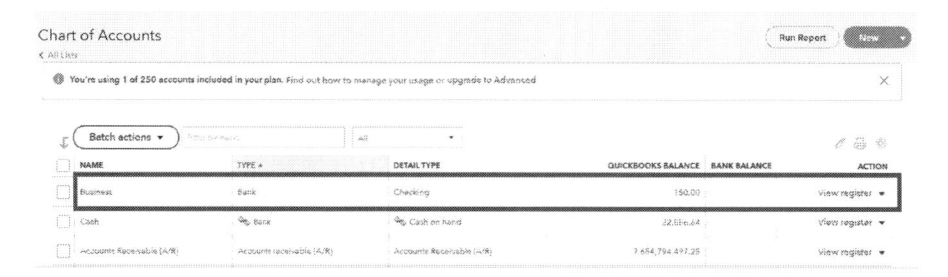

3. Select the **Invoice Payment** you want to edit and click the **Edit** button.

4. This process redirects you to Receive Payment. Tick the box next to the invoice number in Outstanding Transactions.

5. Select **Save and close**.

09

TAXES

For the services and products, you provide, there might be a need for you to collect sales tax from customers. Use QuickBooks to keep track of your tax obligations so you can pay your dues on time and avoid penalties.

QuickBooks has a built-in feature that calculates sales tax for you automatically, so you can file your returns without any guesswork. The program alerts you about the next tax deadline so that you may submit punctually and avoid penalties.

To accurately close your books as tax filing season approaches, you must have kept good records throughout the year. QB Online streamlines your accounting processes to help you efficiently file your taxes in preparation of the upcoming tax season.

ADDING VAT

Value-added tax (VAT) is a type of sales tax that is charged to consumers at any point in the manufacturing or distribution of a product or service when additional value is created. QuickBooks has a built-in feature that automatically calculates VAT for you, so you can file your taxes with confidence. Get VAT set up and running to simplify your tax preparation.

1. Setting up a tax. For certain countries, adding custom tax rates is available. QuickBooks may have your taxes set up depending on your region. To set up a tax agency:

1. Click **VAT** then click **Set up VAT**.

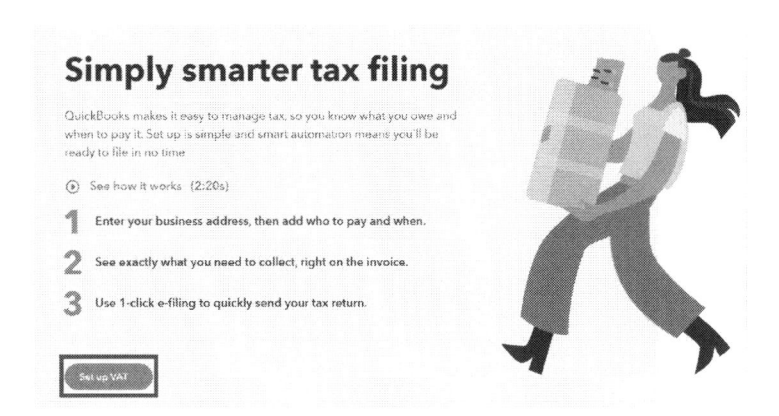

2. Add the **Tax name, Description, Tax agency name**.

3. Select a **Start of current tax period**.

4. Select a tax **Filing frequency** for **VAT**.

5. Select a **Reporting Method**.

6. Click **Next** then **OK**.

2. Assign a VAT category to a product or service. This lets QuickBooks know how much VAT you need to charge based on precisely what you're selling.

   1. Click **Get paid & pay** and select **Products and services**.

   2. Find the item you want to categorize as a tax, then select **Edit**.

3. Click the **TAX** dropdown, then look up and select the precise VAT rate for your item.

4. **Save and close**.

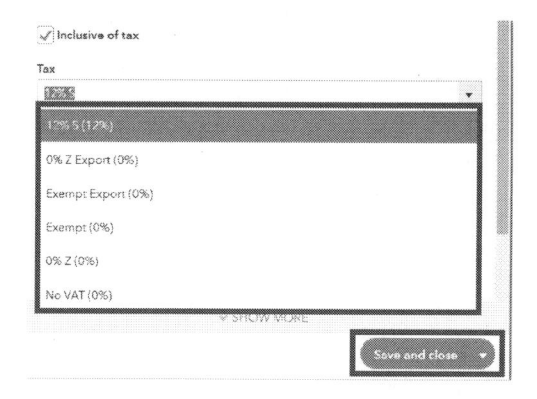

3. After everything is set up, you may begin applying taxes in your sales form and invoice.

1. Create an invoice or sales receipt, follow the steps as instructed in previous chapters.

2. Ensure location of sale and add other necessary information.

3. Check the **Tax** column for your taxable items.

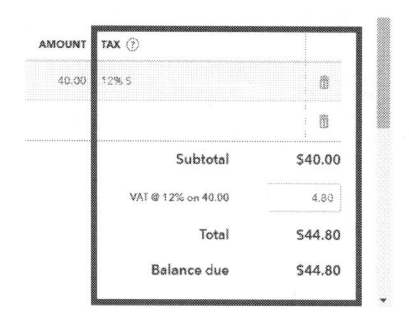

4. Click **Save and send**.

CREATING AND FILING 1099S

For federal income tax purposes, non-salary income is reported to the IRS on Form 1099, an "information filing form." A 1099-NEC is a type of 1099 forms filed if you paid an independent contractor more than $600 in a given tax year.

The IRS and your contractors must receive 1099s by January 31. However, before January 27 at 5:00 PM PT, we advise you to file electronically. Before doing this, you can guarantee that your contractors will receive their 1099s by January 31. To submit your 1099s electronically on time to the IRS, you have until January 31.

You may prepare your 1099s using the data you already have in your accounts with the help of a time-saving function in QuickBooks Online. You can mail a printed copy of your 1099s to your contractors in addition to preparing and submitting them, so they can use it for their tax filing.

Setting up 1099

To easily set up your 1099 account, make sure to only choose "non-employee compensation" for contractor payments. If not, you might need to modify the payments you make to your contractors and accounts.

1. Click **Payroll** menu and select **Contractors**.
2. Click **Prepare 1099s**.

3. Click **Continue you 1099s**.

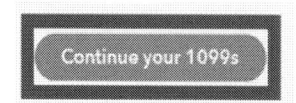

4. Review your company info such as **Name and address**, **Phone number** and **Tax ID**. Click the **pencil icon** to edit. Click **Next** to continue.

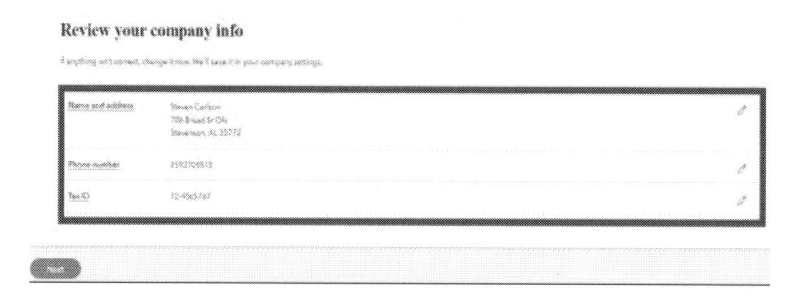

5. Select the boxes that indicate contractor payments, then click **Next**. Note that selecting your boxes may apply changes to the 1099 forms. The majority of businesses will select "Non-employee compensation" (Box 1 1099-NEC), but if you believe you may have made other types of payments, check with your accountant.

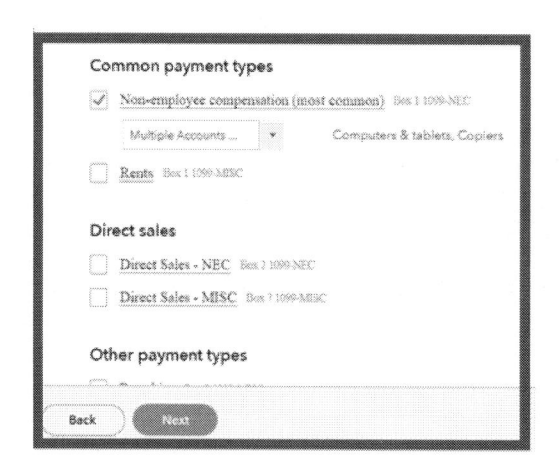

6. Make sure all of the personal information of your contractors is accurate. Click **Edit** under the **Actions** column to update any information. Click **Next**.

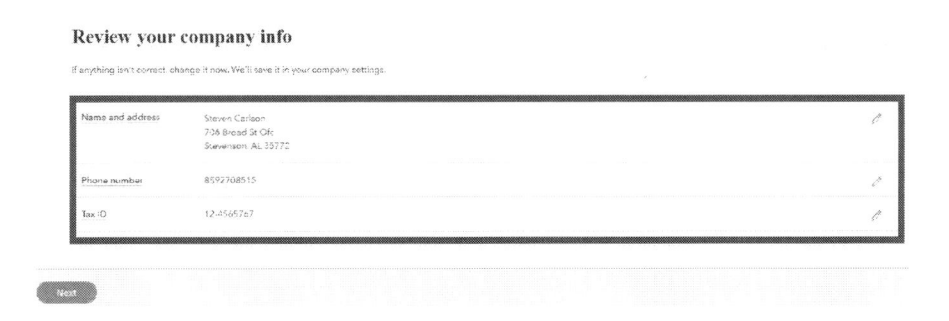

7. Check that the payments for contractors add up. Click the dropdown the select 1099 contractors filter to verify your 1099 filing.

8. If happy with the information, click **Finish preparing 1099s**

E-Filing of 1099

Your 1099 is now ready for filing on January 1. QuickBooks will e-file 1099 with the IRS on your behalf and will also deliver 1099 to your contractors electronically. This will be available for a view in an Intuit account for free. Lastly, the copies of the 1099 will be printed and mailed by QuickBooks to your contractors.

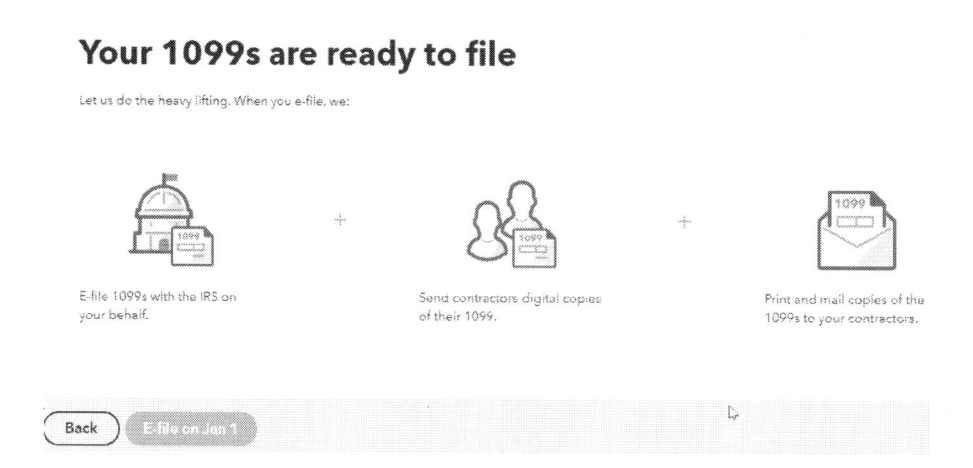

Your 1099s are ready to file

Let us do the heavy lifting. When you e-file, we:

E-file 1099s with the IRS on your behalf.   +   Send contractors digital copies of their 1099.   +   Print and mail copies of the 1099s to your contractors.

Back   E-file on Jan 1

9. If you want to print and mail 1099 yourself, click **No, I'll print and mail** at the bottom right. Follow the simple steps on the screen to print and mail 1099.

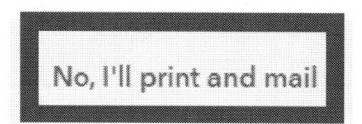

No, I'll print and mail

10
REPORTS

With its robust reports feature, QuickBooks makes it easier for you to locate information about your business. You can find a consistent display in the reports, which will both assist you in learning how to read the reports and make it simple for you to discover details of your business.

You have the option to create simple reports, create and save customized reports, apply filters, and view layouts of your choice, and export reports to professional file formats. When you do this, it will be much simpler for you to put together business documents, which you can then use for either presentations or documentation.

The Reports Center of the software contains a range of preconfigured QuickBooks reports that provide information about many aspects of your company. These reports mostly focus on financial matters.

TYPES OF REPORT

The different types of statements you can access to help you analyze your business performance are the following:

1. Transaction reports compile your financial dealings in a variety of forms to help you quickly access the data you need to run your company. Every company relies on a select few essential reports, such as Profit & Loss Report, Balance Sheet, A/R Aging Summary, A/P Aging Summary, and General Ledger. Here is a look at a transaction report.
2. List reports provide you information about the various lists available in QuickBooks including:
    A. **Chart of Accounts** - shows a list of accounts and detail types with account balances

B. **Customer List** – reports on list of customer information like full name, phone number, email address, as well as billing and shipping address

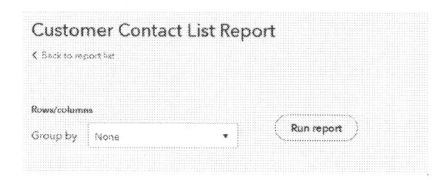

C. **Supplier List** - reports on list of supplier information like full name, phone number, email address, and address

3. **Summary Reports -** You may get summary data on clients, sales, costs, and more with the help of summary reports. The report presents data that is summarized. Below is a sample of a summary report.

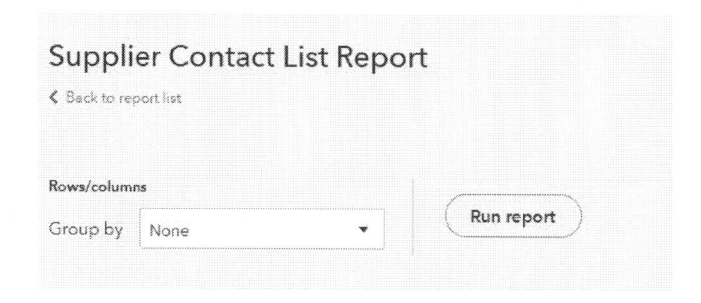

4. **Detail Reports** – Detail reports provide you with specifics about your clients, transactions, expenditures, etc. Detailed data is presented in the report. In contrast to the summaries and totals included in the balance sheet, the detail report lists each transaction that has taken place.

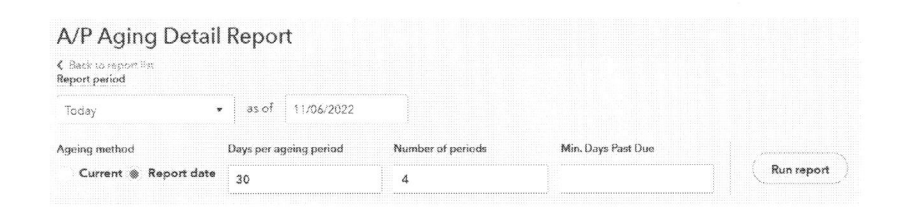

ADD A REPORT AS FAVORITE

The reporting features of QuickBooks help grow your business. You can view the data you want and how you want it shown, thanks to the platform's hundreds of custom and built-in reports.

Favorites are for you if you have a set of reports that you review regularly. Favorites are reports that you have added as favorites because you run and review them often. These favorites are unique to your account and belong to you.

Click the star symbol next to the report's name to mark the report as a favorite.

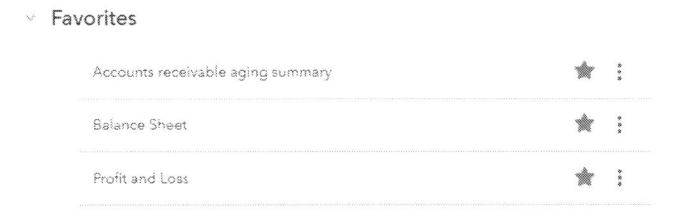

MOST IMPORTANT TYPES OF STATEMENTS

Key Reports for Your Business

The two most important reports for most businesses are (insert how to generate reports for each.)

E. **Profit & Loss Report (Income Statement)** - knowing how well or poorly your firm did within a certain time frame is easy with the help of the profit and loss statement. You can view at a glance whether you are making or losing money when reviewing the report, which provides a rundown of your revenue and expenditures over the course of a particular period.

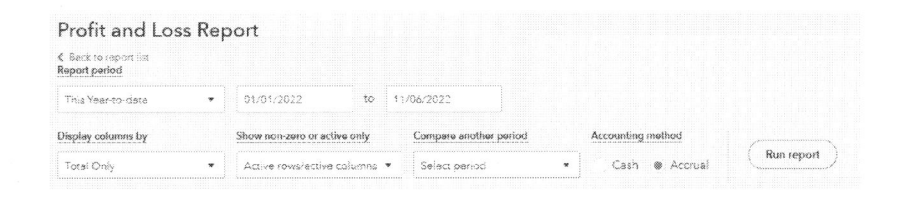

How to run a profit and loss report:

6. 1. Click **Reports**.

7. 2. Go to **Business Overview** and click **Profit & Loss**.

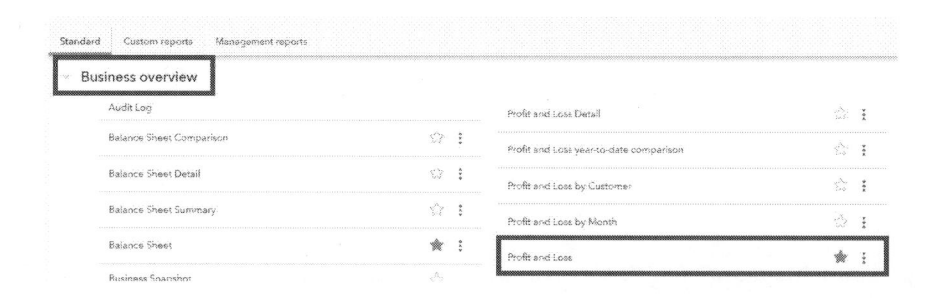

B. **Balance Sheet** - an overview of your company's financial health. By deducting all your company's debts (liabilities) from its assets (assets), the report concludes at your equity (assets).

How to run a profit and loss report:

3. Click **Reports**.

4. Go to **Business Overview** and click **Balance Sheet**.

C. **A/R Aging Summary** - accounts receivable details the outstanding balances for each overdue client, including the total amount owed for the current billing cycle, any unpaid amounts from previous cycles, and any outstanding balances for specific jobs.

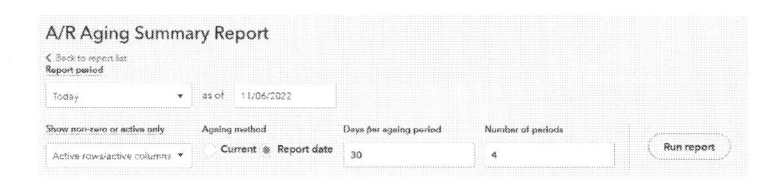

How to run a profit and loss report:

1. Go to **Reports**.
2. Go to **Who owes you**. Click **A/R Aging Summary**.

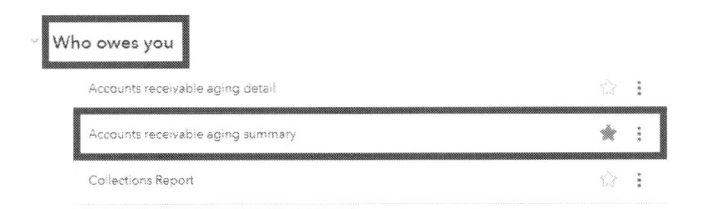

D. **A/P Aging Summary** - reports your accounts payable balance, outstanding bills, and creditors. The report displays how much your business owes each supplier for the current and past billing periods.

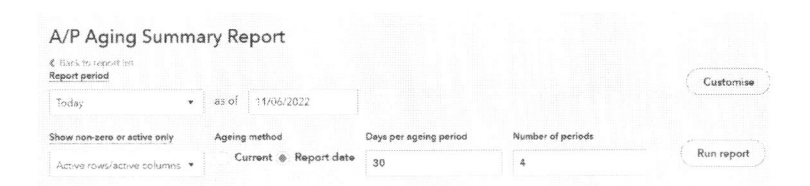

How to run a profit and loss report:

1. Click **Reports**.
2. Go to **What you owe section**.
3. Click **A/P Aging Summary**.

D. **Accounting Reports** - reports you should provide your accountant so they may evaluate your records, create, and send personalized financial reports in accordance with the demands of your business. You'll find important reports for you and your accountant, such as:

1. The **Journal report** - details all debits and credits for a certain time period in order.

2. The **General Ledger** - records all the transactions that have been made in an account where each account's starting balance is included.

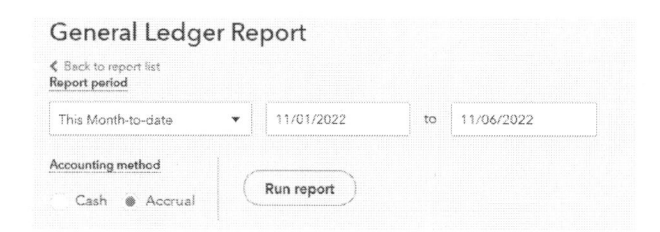

3. **Transaction List by Date** - If you need to go over all of your transactions in chronological order, this report will be a big support.

HOW TO CUSTOMIZE REPORTS

Any type of report you want to run in QuickBooks may be customized.

You may make use of pre-existing report templates in a number of ways to create a more unique accounting report. The good news is that making a customized report will be simple if you know how to make reports in QuickBooks.

The data may be altered by adding or removing columns, changing data filters, and adding or removing header and footer information. On each report that you send, you may also decide to switch the format from portrait to landscape and even include remarks.

Finally, you may save customized reports in QuickBooks Online for later use or mark them as favorites for quick access.

1. Start by opening the report you want to edit. Click **Customize**.

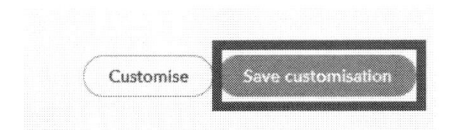

2. Click the **General dropdown**, enter the **Report Period, Accounting method, Number format, Negative numbers**. Tick the box if you want to show negative numbers in red.

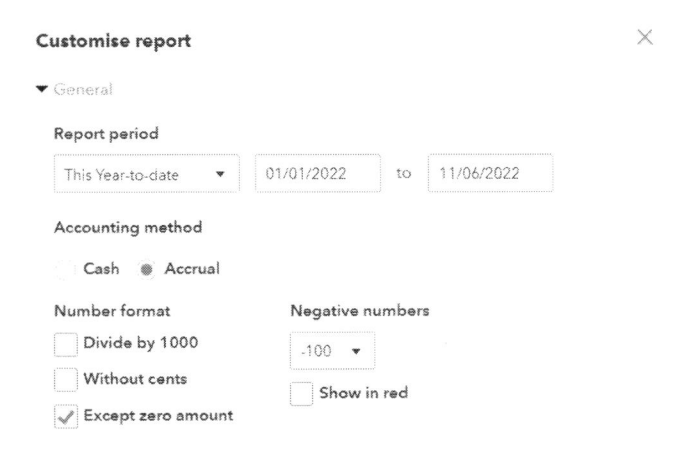

3. To broaden the selections for the report presentation, click **Rows/Columns dropdown**. Choose which columns to include in the report. Select if you want your rows and columns to **Show non-zero or active only**. You also have the option to change and reorder columns by selecting a column checkbox.

4. Under Filters dropdown, select your preference on how you want to display your Customer, Supplier and Product/Service.

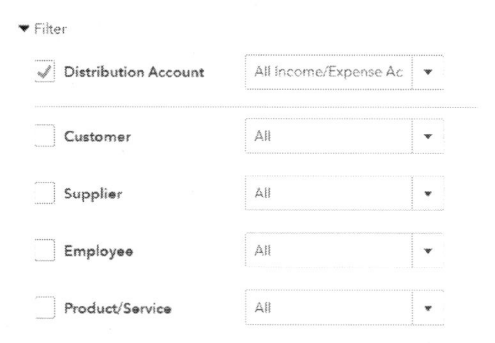

5. Click the **Header/Footer dropdown**. Choose the details that will appear in the report's header and footer. Select the **Alignment** if required.

6. Select **Run Report**. The report that QuickBooks displays includes the header, footer, filters, columns, and rows that you choose.

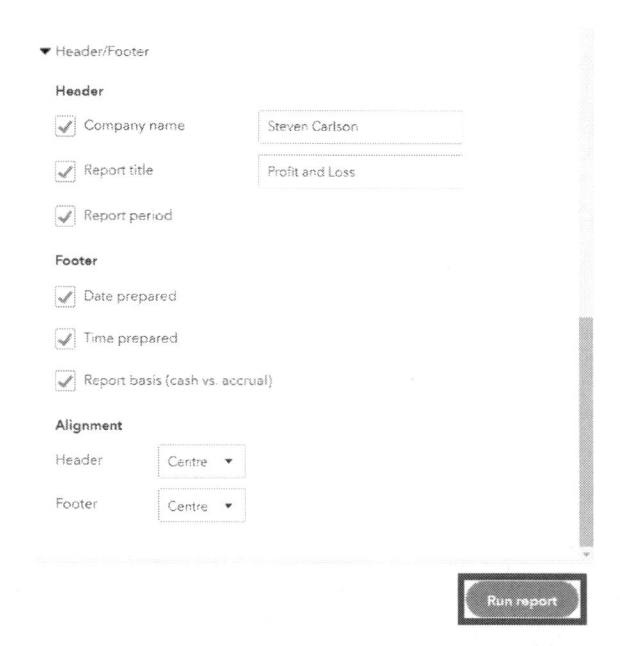

Save custom reports

You may save a QuickBooks report's customization to easily replicate later. When you customize a report, you may save it in **My Custom Reports List**. When you need a duplicate report, navigate to **My Custom Reports List**.

1. On the top right, click **Save customization**.

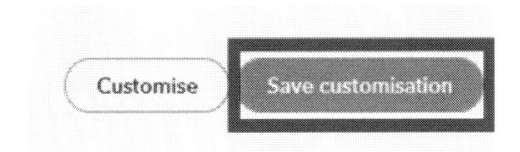

2. Enter the **Custom** report name and other information you want to add.
3. Click **Save**.

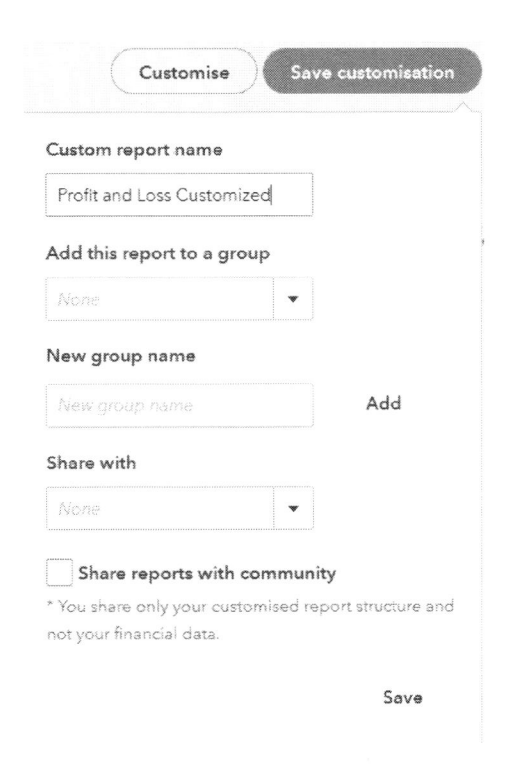

QuickBooks saves report settings that are created. It adds the custom report to the **Custom reports** tab.

1. Click **Reports**, then click the **Custom reports** tab.
2. Select the report from the list.

11
TROUBLE SHOOTING

There are many fun things you can do using QuickBooks however, without proper user guidance, using the accounting software may cause some severe issues, even though it is intended to make things as easy as possible. In this case, you will discover the most typical QuickBooks mistakes in this chapter, along with advice on how to fix them. Knowing what these errors are can help you maintain your books correctly while saving time and preventing any tension they may create.

MOST COMMON ERRORS IN QUICKBOOKS AND HOW TO FIX THEM

1. Incorrectly categorized bank transactions

The fact that your balance matches the bank's does not guarantee that all transactions were recorded accurately. You might not get accurate reports if you have transactions that are not categorized properly. The good news is, you can still make corrections to a banking transaction even after it has been reconciled. To change your transaction category:

1. Click the **Accounting** menu and select **Chart of Accounts**.
2. Click bank account where you want to change a transaction, then click **Account History**.

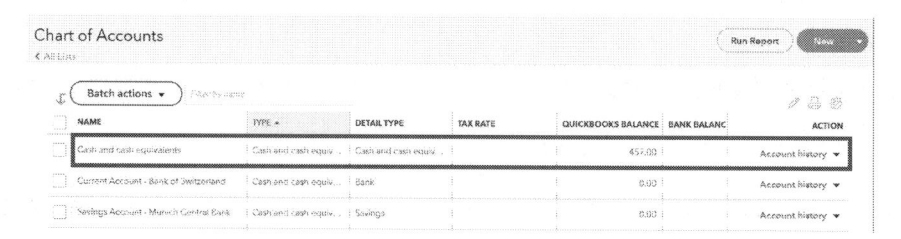

3. Find the transaction you want to edit, select it, then click **Edit**.

4. Change the category accordingly. Click **Save and close**.

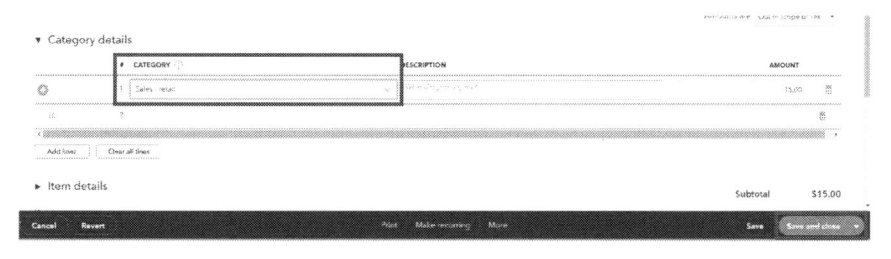

5. Click **Yes** to confirm the changes.

6. Go to **Reports** and run a **Profit and Loss report**.

7. Scan the list to check if your transactions are correctly categorized.

2. Not Using the Purchase Order

You can use the tools in QuickBooks Online to handle sales, including purchasing, but many business owners don't take advantage of this very helpful system. Purchase orders list the items and the quantity you want to buy from a vendor. When you're ready to buy products, you can make a purchase order (PO) and send it to a vendor.

When you create a PO every time you buy from a supplier, you can also create an accurate list of items and their quantities, which you can then review carefully. You can also enter your PO quickly to a transaction for an expense or bill in QuickBooks so that all your transactions are linked, and your accounts are balanced. Just make sure find the items according to your PO. To start using a Purchase Order, follow these steps:

Set up purchase order in QuickBooks

1. Click **Settings** then click **Account and settings**.
2. Click **Expenses**.
3. Click the **pencil icon** in the **Purchase orders** section.

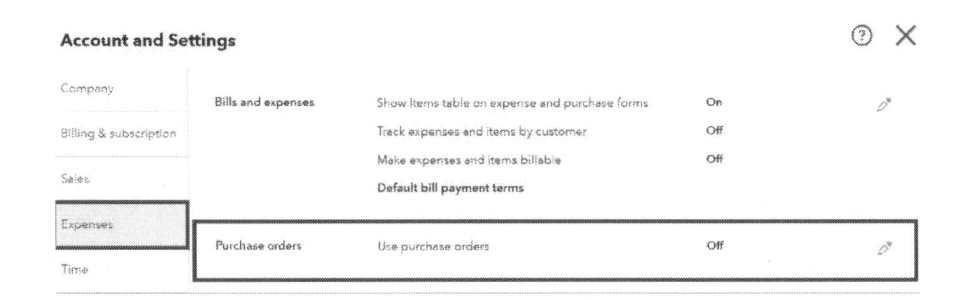

4. Activate **Use purchase orders**.

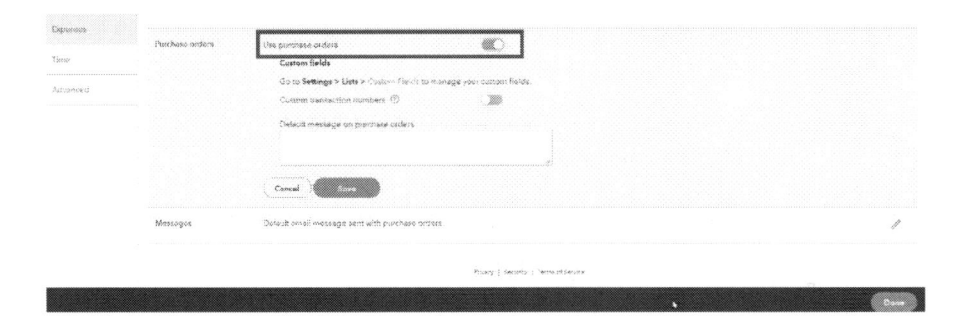

5. Click **Save**, then click **Done**.

Create a purchase order

1. Click **+New** then click **Purchase order**.
2. Select a supplier from the Supplier menu and verify the mailing address.
3. Click the **Ship to dropdown** then **Ship via** if you are sending the items directly to a consumer.
4. Type the **date of the Purchase Order**.

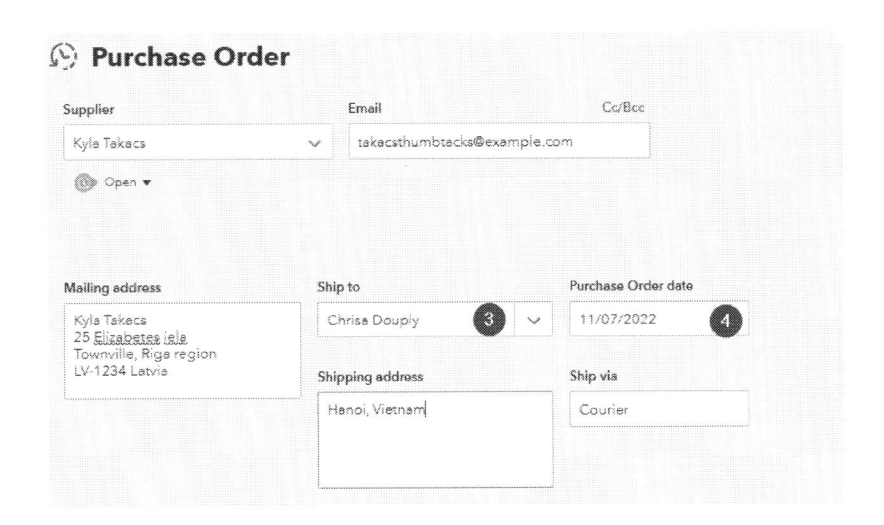

5. Click **Settings** on the **Purchase Order** form.

6. Next, create your own custom fields in the **Choose what you use** section.

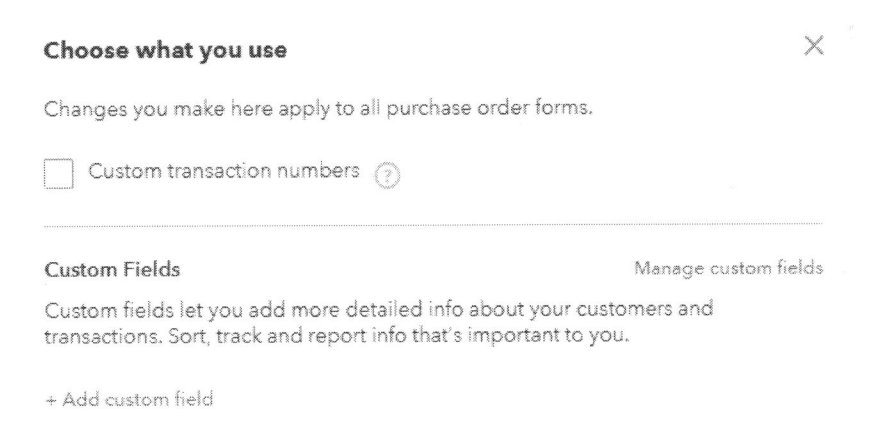

7. Enter the items you want to buy in the **Item details** section.

Trouble Shooting

8. Select **Save and close** or **Save and send** if you're ready to send the purchase order to your supplier.

3. Improper deposit slip printing

To keep a physical record of transactions, you may print the deposit slip from QuickBooks. Setting up the deposit slip will assist you in printing it in the proper manner so that it covers the whole pre-printed form space. If you have problems printing deposit slips with information that does not line up with the proper areas of the form, we may have a solution for this.

Setting up a print deposit slip

Printing a sample deposit slip and comparing it to the deposit slip form is the first step in setting up a deposit slip printing. Use a blank paper as a sample printing.

1. Click **+New**.
2. Click on **Bank deposit** under Other section.
3. Click **Print**.
4. To access the setup page for **Print deposit slip**, click **Setup and alignment**.

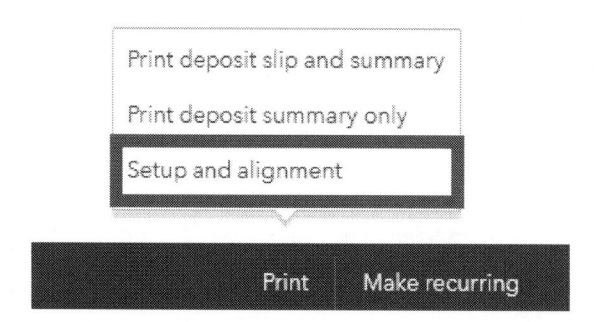

```
Print deposit slip and summary
Print deposit summary only
Setup and alignment
```

```
Print    Make recurring
```

5. Click **View preview and Print sample**.

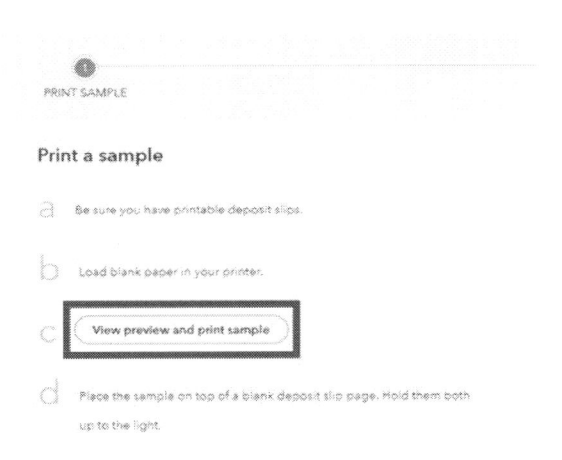

6. Click **Print**.

7. Hold both pre-printed forms up to the light with your printed sample deposit slip on top.

8. In the Print box, click **Yes, I'm finished with setup** if the printed information matches with the appropriate parts of the form. If not, select **No, continue with setup**, and carry through the setup.

QuickBooks may continue to suggest a couple of workarounds to successfully print a deposit slip.

4. Typical login mistakes in QuickBooks Online

Messages like "Web page cannot be found" or "Error 404: File not found" are common error displays that don't let you sign into QuickBooks Online. In this case, you can try these solutions to help you with these kinds of issues.

Option 1: Make sure QuickBooks Online is compatible with your browser first. Among the browser settings required by QuickBooks Online for its pages to load are JavaScript and pop-up windows, so ensure that they are on.

Option 2: Your browser's cache and cookies are used by QuickBooks Online to speed up performance, however, they can prevent online pages from loading. Sign into QuickBooks Online after deleting your cookies and cache.

Option 3: QuickBooks Online may be restricted by your device's security. Add these URLs to the trusted sites list in your browser, then launch your browser again.

- https://qbo.intuit.com
- https://quickbooks.intuit.com/

Option 4: Do a quick restart of your computer and internet modem. Switch off your internet modem and computer and unplug your routers or servers. Turn on your device and modem, then connect your router or server after waiting for a while. After starting up your computer, go onto QuickBooks Online.

CONCLUSION

QuickBooks is an accounting application that is known to be one of the most powerful yet user-friendly. It is used by small companies and large corporations alike. If you're unfamiliar with QuickBooks or if you're a busy person, it will be difficult to learn all of its features. This is why we've put together this guide on how to use QuickBooks online.

QuickBooks Online for Beginners, Updated Edition, takes you step-by-step through all you need to know to begin using QuickBooks Online. This book is ideal for company owners or first-time users who are still learning about accounting and bookkeeping topics. Enjoy full details in simple instructions to help you use this fantastic cloud accounting program.

This book starts by giving an overview of what QuickBooks is and which version of QuickBooks Online is best for you. Then, it goes through the fundamentals of how it works to give you a better idea of what it can do for your company. These contain explanations of features and menus to assist you in navigating the application.

It also walks you through the basic accounting elements of QuickBooks Online, such as automating bank connections, managing expenses and suppliers, invoicing, recording payments while tracking sales, and adding payroll to your QuickBooks account, to get you started efficiently. The second half covers inventory tracking and building projects, as well as a guide to paying taxes and running reports that provide insight into your financial position.

This book is split into chapters that are mostly required when you first begin using QuickBooks Online. The chapters are divided into sections to make it easier for you to digest the information. Also, illustrations are used to highlight any menus or options that must be clicked in line with the directions and to minimize misunderstanding. The procedures are stated in a basic and straightforward way, in which even young students may follow.

This tool may be used by anybody, from a carpenter to a professional service provider, to run their business. QuickBooks Online for Beginners, Updated Edition, contains everything you need to get started with QuickBooks Online and keep your books correct.

Thank You!

This is a quick message of thanks that you picked my book from dozens of other books available for you to purchase.

Thank you for getting this and reading this all the way to the end.

Before you go, I'd like to ask a minute of your time to leave me a review on Amazon. As an indie author, every review (or star rating) matters as it helps our books become more visible on the platform thus in turn helps us reach and help more people.

Scan the QR Codes for your convenience:

US **UK** **CA**

Manufactured by Amazon.ca
Bolton, ON